New Orleans
Ghosts

Victor C. Klein

ISBN   1-880365-66-9

Library of Congress Catalog Card Number   97-666331

Published by Lycanthrope Press
PO Box 9028
Metairie, LA 70005-9028
L. Talbot, senior editor

Dedication

To Persephone whose beauty intrigues us

Table of Contents

French Quarter

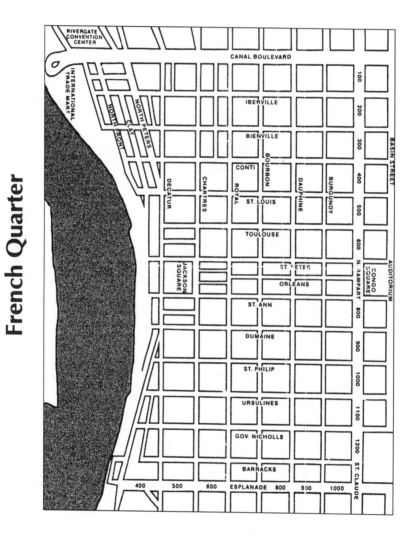

Introduction

New Orleans is probably the most haunted city in the United States.[1] Despite this claim, there has not been a book exclusively devoted to the ghosts and hauntings of the Crescent City since Jean de Lavigne's classic work, *Ghost Stories of Old New Orleans*[2] (1946). *New Orleans Ghosts* is an attempt to fill that void.

There have been many changes in New Orleans in almost five decades. Many of the old haunted houses have been torn down in the name of progress. Forests and woods that once held phantoms and spirits have been replaced by suburbs and skyscrapers. Swamps that guarded secrets better not known have been drained and paved. The ghosts that inhabited these places have vanished. Still, there are numerous haunted houses and spirit-infested areas to be documented. *New Orleans Ghosts* is about such environs. All of the buildings and other places described in this work are easily accessible and still standing as of this writing (1991). Also, the stories have been fully documented and the author has investigated all of the sites in order to add authority to the effort. Maps, diagrams, addresses and photographs have been included to facilitate finding the ghosts whose stories are contained in this book.

This is a serious work which includes a critical analysis of each story. In one instance, the author disproved an old story which, for years, had been accepted as true. On other occasions, the author has raised more questions than he has answered.

Besides serving as a guide to ghosts, this book is also an anthropological work in which are collected documented myths and legends which form an important, if often neglected, component of the Crescent City's unique folklore and traditions. By understanding the myths and concepts upon which a culture is based, we come face to face with the themes that have supported human activity and structured civilization. Our myths have informed our religions, given meaning to individual lives, and created directions for our sundry faiths.[3] This phenomenon - myth - puts our conscious mind in touch with the spirit of humanity - a spirit within each of us. By reflecting on this folklore we learn something about our fears, our faith, our common basis for being human. It is from this that we learn about ourselves, and can better understand and accept ourselves and others as individuals, and as members of the human community.

Finally, we may say that New Orleans has never been an average American big city. Historically, it is a Latin culture flavored with the mystery and misery of the African Negro carried into bondage. Voodoo, gris-gris, All Saint's Day, the Yellow Death, slavery and the Roman Catholic Church all have roots in the fertile, rich bayou soil of New Orleans which go deeper and hold faster than in poorer soil. New Orleans, which has been home and then grave, to so many nationalities, races, and beliefs, has offered American culture and folklore an almost enchanted mystique. Is it no wonder that perhaps the dead may walk here a bit more stealthily than in some more mundane metropolis?

The Flaming Tomb

In the predawn mist that blankets the houses of the dead, a succubus reaches out to the gates of hell. Her cold hand slams against the heavy metal doors. The thunderous sound echoes off the still, mute tombs that lay at her back. Without warning the portal belches forth a demon red flame whose glow ignites the white sepulchers with a crimson fury. Slowly, she turns to face the city of the dead from Satan's Roost. Her eyes reflect the glowing nimbus of the she wolf as she glides from the flaming doors to prowl.

She is of delicate beauty given animation by passions who know not death. Under her dainty feet the grass withers as she begins her periodic sojourn into the bleak night. Woe to the hapless transient who seeks a night's repose in her cemetery. Pity the foolish thrill seeker who brazenly trespasses in her domain. Death would be a blessing to whomever witnesses her wanderings. It is said that those whose eyes find her dwell in madness until Mephistopheles drags them into the abyss and an eternity of cruel sufferings.

She is the bride of Satan. She is the Madam of Storyville. She is Josie Arlington.[1]

One of New Orleans best known ghost stories has as its origin the death and burial of a Mrs. Josie Deubler, a.k.a. Josie Arlington. Josie was New Orleans' most colorful and infamous madam. From 1897 to 1917 New Orleans was the site of America's largest and most successful experiment in legalized prostitution. Up until 1897 prostitution thrived in virtually every section of the city that care forgot. This over abundance of women selling what men wanted most concerned the city fathers. Realizing that the practice could never be obliterated it was wisely decided to contain and control the ladies of the night. The best plan was voiced by Alderman Sidney Story. Under Story's plan, thirty-eight square blocks were designated a restricted district where prostitution could flourish and be controlled. Much to the dismay of Alderman Story, the district was christened with his name and became forever known as Storyville.

It was from this city within a city that Josie Arlington practiced her profession and grew rich, very, very rich. Josie operated perhaps the finest bordello in the district. Beautiful women, fine liquors, delicious food and exotic drugs all found a great demand at Josie's. Women and girls frocked in Parisian lingerie greeted both the gentlemen and not-so-gentle men of New Orleans.

Beautiful Josie could count the cream of New Orleans society as her customers. Landowners and politicians, judges and lawyers, bankers and physicians all found a haven with Josie and her girls. In the confines of the Arlington, Josie's bordello, these men found what was lacking in their staid Victorian homes. Here a man could exercise his fantasies or just relax without baleful stares or whiplike tongues shamelessly assaulting his dignity. In these walls was the comfort of the marriage bed without its attendant discipline.

Josie was a monarch in her world. She had the attention, and yes, even the love and friendship of many of the most influential and powerful men in the city. But Josie was denied the one thing she most wanted - social acceptance. She knew many important men better than their wives; however, these very families shunned and despised her for her honesty. Her money and charm meant nothing to the society she longed to embrace.

Even though life had deprived her of the social standing she so desired, that did not end her aspirations or her hatred for the world that both encouraged and condemned her. What she could not have in life she would have in death. Josie exacted her vengeance by electing to be buried in the city's most fashionable cemetery - Metairie Cemetery.

She purchased a plot and raised a small hill where she erected an ornate red marble tomb topped by two blazing pillars. She commissioned Albert Weiblen, one of the city's most prestigious designers of funerary architecture.[2] He created a masterpiece from the red Stonington, Maine marble.[3] The tomb, rising from its hillock, surveyed the graves of many men she had once known in life. On the steps leading to her final resting place she commissioned an F. Bagdon to create a beautiful bronze statue who ascended the stairs, bouquet of roses in the crook of her arm. The statue, as it is placed, has her back turned to the family graves which surround her. As these families turned their back to Josie in life, so would she, in death, return the favor.

Needless to say, the tomb and statue caused a virtual scandal. One can imagine a nagging wife's exclaiming, "it was bad enough that Papa knew 'that woman' in life, but to lie with her in death as well is absolutely hideous." Josie was avenged.

No sooner had the tomb and statue been finished in 1911 than a strange story began to race through the city. Some curiosity seekers had driven out to see the tomb and, of course, express their dismay. Upon their arrival one evening they were greeted by a sight that set them scurrying. The tomb seemed to burst into flames before their shocked eyes. The smooth red marble played host to a bewildering array of flames that danced and snaked their way along its surface.[4] The sepulchre quickly became the talk of the town. Droves of people came to stare in morbid fascination at the flaming tomb. The cemetery administrators, the bereaved families, the entire metropolis was in a state of shock over this bizarre occurrence. Scandal followed Josie even to death.

A burning tomb resembling the gates of hell heralding the entrance of a scarlet woman was bad enough, but Josie was not yet finished with her vengeance. She died in 1914, and was promptly buried in her rosy grave. Almost from the exact day of her burial an alarming number of sightseers began to relate a second weird event. Many swore that they had actually seen the statue move. The report of the animated bronze statue reached a startling climax when two of the cemetery sextons, a Mr. Todkins and a Mr. Anthony, swore that they had both witnessed the statue's leaving her post and move stealthily among the tombs.[5] The sextons, displaying more courage than sense, followed her as she strolled down a serpentine shell road and suddenly disappeared. The tradition of the Flaming Tomb has been kept alive as part of New Orleans occult heritage in several books,[6] and as varying, garbled oral traditions.

In order to shed light on this classic ghost story I interviewed Mr. Henri Gandalfo, author of *Metairie Cemetery*,[7] and an employee of the cemetery for over sixty years. He explained that the apparent flames were nothing more than the reflection of a swaying light that once marked a toll road that ran parallel to the cemetery. When the light was removed in the 1920's the phenomenon ended. Mr. Gandalfo also categorically denied the stories which credited the statue with nightly sojourns among the dead.

On the surface, it would appear that this tale is nothing more than a legend combined with superstition equalling a "ghost story." Ordinarily I would tend to accept this explanation if it was not for two peculiar instances which transpired while doing research for this story. In early March of 1986 I visited the site in order to copy names, dates, etc. I was accompanied by a friend, Carolyn Albritton, who was interested in the story and the personality behind the legend. While kneeling at the foot of the statue copying the sculpture's name, my friend yelled out and lunged forward. Immediately, I looked up to see the statue's falling in my direction. I reached up with both hands as my friend arrived to add her arm and shoulder to the task. With no small effort we returned the statue to her traditional location. The statue weighs several hundred pounds. For over seventy years it could not have been so liable to tip over that it would not have been destroyed years ago. The day of our investigation was calm and mild. Neither of us felt any type of tremor or disturbance that could have accounted for our lady's sudden desire to embrace this author. I returned several subsequent times, alone, but nothing noteworthy transpired. For all intents and purposes, the tomb, apart from its obvious beauty, was like all of its neighbors, silent through the mystery of death.

During February of 1987 I was speaking with Carolyn, who had accompanied me on that coincidental day from the previous year. Noting that Friday the 13th fell in the month of February, she felt it would be auspicious for us to again visit the site (and it was a full moon). We arrived in a lighthearted, jovial air more akin to two college pranksters, rather than as paranormal researchers. It was approximately 11:30 P.M., 12 February. The moon was full. The sky partly cloudy. It was unseasonably warm. We kept vigil at the tomb, alternately talking, meditating, watching. After two hours during which mediumistic contact was attempted but failed, we became somewhat frustrated and bored. We began to move away from the site. About forty-five feet from the grave on a winding road leading to the old main entrance we became aware of a flashing red light. Later, we discovered we had a simultaneous thought - the police. We were in a closed and locked cemetery at 2:00 A.M. on Friday the 13th during a full moon. I'm positive our discovery would have warranted a trip downtown with the possibility of some bored reporter, on an otherwise unnews-

worthy day, having a first page byline chronicling our exploits. We immediately hid. We ran through a row of tombs that brought us off the road to a less accessible and visible footpath. As we tried to gain intelligence about the light - where was it, was it moving, if moving in what direction and most importantly, who was responsible for it in the first place? We realized the light's origin was in the very area where Josie's monument stands. We ran in the general direction of the light but because of the darkness and the maze-like configuration of the tombs we hit several dead ends before we were once again standing before the Flaming Tomb. Whoever or whatever was responsible for approximately sixty seconds of flashing red light had vanished. Had it been a police car, where was it? The car could have turned right or left, but each one of those directions would betray the cars lights or motion which was undetected by either of us. A second time Carolyn and I left the cemetery perplexed and more than a bit astonished.

La Maison Lalaurie

For almost one-hundred fifty years New Orleanians have referred to the ancient dwelling of Dr. and Madame Lalaurie as the most famous haunted abode in the city. For many natives, the Lalaurie house is the sacred cow of parochial ghost stories. The restored, historically acknowledged home is reputed to hold a virtual pantheon of paranormal horrors - or so say a plethora of sources and convinced local residents. Many guidebooks[1] and the colorful drivers of the omnipresent French Quarter tourist carriages all relate tales of horror and hauntings that still exist behind the thick masonry walls of the elegant, old town-house.

The origin of this famous and widespread spook yarn allegedly dates from 10 April 1834.[2] On that fateful day a fire broke out in the kitchen. The fire spread rapidly and was incapable of being extinguished by the many slaves of the Lalaurie household. In due time the fire brigade arrived with their wagons and hoses. After a heroic effort the blaze was brought under control. As the firemen inspected the property for hidden pockets of resistance they came upon an attic room whose entrance was sealed by a heavily barred door. Fearing that the room might harbor the embers of a yet discovered conflagration the men forced the door. Almost immediately

their nostrils were assailed by the pungent odor of death. As their eyes became adjusted to the dark cavern-like chamber, they reeled and vomited from utter revulsion. The dim room held more than half a dozen chained and bound slaves. Some were dead. Others were in such a state of torment and mutilation as to make death seem a human blessing.

The slaves were both male and female. Some were fastened to the walls with cruel chains. Others were restrained on makeshift operating tables. Still others were confined in metal cages hardly large enough for an average size dog. Laying helter-skelter were human body parts and pails containing organs and severed heads. Haphazardly arranged on the

shelves which hung from the back wall were scientific speci-
men jars holding grizzly souvenirs appropriated from the
hapless wretches who were sold into slavery to serve the rich
and elegant Lalauries.

The stout firemen fled in disgust to summon the municipal
police. The police arrived with doctors and ambulances from
Charity Hospital. Most of the wretched slaves were dead.
Those that still clung to life were scarcely recognizable as
human beings. One hapless Negress was reduced to a writhing
trunk. Her limbs had been amputated and the majority of flesh
had been surgically pared from her skull. Another woman,
confined in a small cage, had virtually every bone in her body
broken and reset at obscene angles. She appeared to be more
crab-like than human. Hanging from a gore splattered wall was
what was left of a large Negro male. He had been castrated in
a fashion which seemed to suggest that he had been the victim
of a crude sex change experiment. Others had parts of their
jaws and facial features so mutilated that they resembled
gargoyles. The dead were fortunate for their torments had been
silenced by the cold embrace of death.

A contemporary account from the issue of the Bee dated 11
April 1834 gives some glimpse as to what the officials discovered. "Seven slaves, more or less horribly mutilated, were seen
suspended by the neck, with their limbs apparently stretched
and torn from one extremity to the other. . . These slaves. . .
had been confined by the woman Lalaurie for several months
in the situation from which they had thus providentially been
rescued, and had been merely kept in existence to prolong their
sufferings, and to make them taste all that the most refined
cruelty could inflict . . ."[3]

Such horror as beheld by the officials who witnessed the
shameless atrocities cannot long be kept silent. Descriptions of
the garret room obscenities raced through the bustling French
Quarter. Every tongue told a different tale, each more horrify-

ing and graphic than the one which had given it birth. Within the hour an outraged and aghast mob had gathered. Torches were set ablaze. Ropes were fashioned ending in the lethal hangman's noose. The crowd screamed for vengeance, for blood, for justice. Abruptly, a carriage fired through the mighty gates of the mansion. In a cloud of dust four frenzied horses pulled a shuttered, black carriage through the blood crazed mob. Within a matter of moments the suspect Lalaurie family had disappeared from sight.

Neither Madame Lalaurie nor her physician husband were ever seen again. Rumors as to their fate still circulate to this day. Some say the blood thirsty sadists absconded to France. Others maintain that the wicked couple hid themselves among the pine forests on the North Shore of Lake Pontchatrain. Another faction swears that the notorious duo hid themselves in some dark nest of perversion within the city itself. Their exact fate became the substance of many myths and legends.[4]

After the dead, dying and mutilated slaves were removed the house was sacked and vandalized by an outraged citizenry. It became a pariah. No one wanted any association with the vile location. The house remained vacant for many years. It fell into decay and disrepair. Its feral state was maintained by ghastly rumors. Many a solid citizen swore that ungodly screams could be heard in the dark of the moon. Witnesses came forth to testify that parades of mutilated Negroes could be seen gliding along the creaking balconies. Or, that a white woman with a whip accompanied by a blood encrusted man with wolf-like eyes could be glimpsed peering from the attic windows. Stories also circulated about vagrants who, seeking shelter in the forbidden fortress, were never again seen - in one piece!

Some forty years passed before the house was once again occupied. In the 1870's the property became in turn a girls' school and then a music conservatory. During these years the ghosts were silent.

Then in the 1890's a large contingent of Italian immigrants began coming to New Orleans. Many of these new arrivals settled in the French Quarter. For obvious financial reasons the deserted ruin soon became a crowded tenement. Its forty rooms could house forty families who would happily accept almost any accommodations. The old home was quickly animated by the robust Italians. The courtyard and stables came to life with the noises and smells of horses, goats and chickens. Children cavorted in the halls. Men and women made love and dreamed and lived in the cramped rooms.

Almost as soon as the hardy Italians had taken up residence then did a whole new generation of hauntings appear. Men on their way to labor on the waterfront found their mules and horses agonizingly butchered. Decapitated dogs and cats appeared on the dark staircases. Children were occasionally attacked by a white female phantom swinging a blood soaked whip.

One eventful evening a burly longshoreman returned home late from his labors. As he climbed the steep stairs to his stifling apartment he was confronted by a huge Negro male. The man blocking the Italian's path was naked and bound with chains. The longshoreman's powerful hands reached for the intruder. In an instant, the Negro disappeared. By morning so had most of the immigrants.

A barroom and then a furniture store took advantage of the cheap rent. The saloon, owned by an F. Greco, was appropriately named the "Haunted Saloon."[5] Accordingly, Mr. Greco was a fount of "ghost stories" which he swore he and many of his patrons witnessed.[6] The furniture store did not fare as well as the saloon. The owner first suspected vandals when he opened for business one morning to find his wares ruined by gallons of putrid filth. He replaced his merchandise and waited for the vandals with a shotgun. The next morning the new furniture was equally soiled and the owner was close to the edge of insanity. The store closed.

Today the property has been returned to its former elegance. It holds several luxurious apartments. Personal investigations have failed to surface any recent accounts of any unusual activity. For all intents and purposes the only ghosts that now haunt the old Lalaurie home are gossip and fading memories.

A Haunted House

U nlike most of the other haunted places described in this work, it is necessary to keep the location of this house a secret. This is done at the request of the property's owner. The gentleman respects his privacy and does not wish it invaded by would-be ghost hunters. I would not have included this story because I wanted this work, in part, to help other researchers and interested individuals locate these unique sites; however, the story is so remarkable I felt compelled to include it. The facts of this case are of such a frightful and verifiable nature that they contribute positively to my thesis that there are worlds and entities apart from and alien to that which we consider to be the universe.

I can say that the house is located in an old section of uptown New Orleans, a scant few blocks from the Mississippi River. It was constructed in 1832 by a Creole family whose name must remain anonymous. The classic New Orleans style Greek revival mansion was intended as a country home for the prosperous family. Its massive two-story frame boasts 16 spacious rooms, two kitchens (one for summer use, the other for winter), a two-story slave quarter and sundry other buildings for live stock, storage, etc. The 16 rooms are encased in 14 to 18 inch masonry walls, supported on a solid cypress and iron foundation. The house originally stood on several hundred acres of the riverfront woods. Today the lot has been reduced to less than a quarter of an acre.[1] It is within these walls that dwell some of the most active and blood thirsty ghosts in the Crescent City.

The present owner of the house, Mr. J., acquired the property in 1969. At that time, the neighborhood was in a state of decay similar to the looming mansion which hid in its midst. Mr. J. passed the old home on his way to and from work. At first he thought he passed a vacant, overgrown lot. One day he noticed a roof peak riding with the tree tops. Quickly he realized there was a house behind all of the foliage. He remarked that his first encounter with the old dwelling was almost surrealistic. In the ebbing fire of dusk, he beheld a great ghost ship of a house astride the sea of time. He was instantly fascinated. Mr. J. began to inquire after the owner. The gentleman who owned the deserted house said he would willingly sell because of his hatred for it. For eleven years it was vacant. Its last occupant, an eighty-eight year old female recluse had died of starvation in an upstairs bedroom. Her son, the owner, refused to set foot in the house after his mother's bizarre and tragic death. The lovely old mansion stood fallow for over a decade. It became a nest for rats and a roost for pigeons. Vandals invaded. Transients drank, ate and slept within its crumbling walls. What Mr. J. found in 1969 was a 137 year-old mansion that was literally falling down around his ears. Undaunted, he acquired the property and immediately began extensive renovations. During the course of the work, Mr. J. discovered a wealth of finds. Apart from a large stock of furniture and oil paintings, the new owner unearthed a collection of remarkable old diaries. These diaries were to play an important role in providing insights into the occurrences that were to become a chilling part of his life.

The decay and rubble were no surprise. What was a surprise was a room that was markedly different from any of the others. The second story room that was so bewildering was virtually littered with the bones of animals. The remains of dogs and cats, as well as rodents and birds, lay helter-skelter in every nook and cranny of the eldrich enclosure. Upon closer examination, it was discovered that the bones had dried to a brittle whiteness devoid of any skin or flesh. Someone, or something, had seemingly stripped the flesh from those hapless creatures.

Shortly after the renovations had begun, Mr. J. had created enough comfort to begin his residency. While working on plans for the continuing restorations, he felt a presence in the room. He turned from his labors to come face to face with a diminutive, middle-aged woman in a dark period dress. He leaped to his feet and demanded an account from her. She replied by simply vanishing before his eyes. Shaken, the new tenant rushed through the house searching for the woman and securing doors and windows. Several nights later the woman re-appeared and walked right past him into a darkened hall-way. Mr. J. pursued her. He switched on the lights to reveal a hallway that harbored no visual trace. All that lingered were soft footsteps and the faint odor of perfume.

The tiny woman in black has been observed by Mr. J. and his friends several hundred times in the past twenty years. During an interview with the owner on 20 May 1990, he provided me with the following information about this mysterious appari-tion. All of the sightings occur between midnight and dawn. The spectre very seldom interacts with its witnesses. Although on various occasions she has slapped or pushed a number of female guests. She stands between 4'6" and 4'8" in height. She appears opaque and gives every visual appearance of being a normal, albeit short, Caucasian female in her mid-forties. Her footsteps can be heard and her perfume sometimes lingers.

Never has she spoken or uttered any audible sounds. Mr. J. believes she is the unnamed French governess mentioned in the old diaries. According to these sources, she died in the house in 1872 during one of the periodic yellow fever epidemics. It is mentioned that she died, but no information is provided concerning her place of burial. Nor did the diaries reveal any facts about her personal life. She is spoken of as a faithful servant, and very little else. She, just as her appearances, is an enigma.

The next phenomenon which resides in the house is a ghost who confines her activities to a solid wall. The wall in question rejects all objects fastened to it. It also exhibits a dark stain that overcomes all attempts at eradication. The owner, on various occasions, hung pictures and brick-a-brac on the wall in question only to have them dislodged and torn apart. The dark stain has received several sandings, coats of sealer and paint, only to manifest itself time and again despite all efforts to erase it.

The old diaries provide startling data as to the origin of the stain. It seems that a terribly deformed baby was born to the original family. In the middle of the nineteenth century such an unfortunate event was not viewed with much enlightenment. The sad creature was looked upon as a curse from either God or hell to be sequestered until death would purge it from its miserable existence. This was the case with this wretched child. She lived a short, tormented life. Even her death was marked by prejudice and superstition. The family, hoping to preserve its dark secret, decided to bury the child in the flue of a second story fireplace. The deformed body was sealed with mortar and bricks in the chimney. The secret was safe. The child rested, unknown and unseen, in the forgotten fireplace. The only evidence of this anonymous grave is the wall's violent rejection of any profane clutter, and the indelible reddish brown blemish.

In all the annals of ghost stories, it is rare indeed to encounter a ghost or spirit who is intent on violence. The vast majority of supernatural tales usually reveal ghosts who are basically non-interactive with the living beings who are fortunate enough to encounter them. Many ghosts seem content to play out a solitary drama and return to whatever region from which they came.[2] The man in black who also haunts this house is an appalling exception of this rule.

As previously mentioned, the present owner discovered a killing room that held the remains of a substantial number of animals. Again, the old diaries shed some light on this mysterious room and the blood lusting ghoul who still, after more than a century and a half, parades his Satanic madness in its confines. As previously mentioned, the old house is very close to the Mississippi River. In the 1830's and 40's slavery was still legal in the U.S. but not the importation of slaves. The owner of our house in question was a man of great wealth. Some of this wealth was the product of illegal activities. A certain individual referred to in the crumbling diaries as the Black Captain - Noir Captain - smuggled illegal slaves to the riverfront house for distribution to the sprawling plantations that abounded in the area. While the Black Captain conducted his nefarious business in the city he boarded with his Creole partner in the room that held the bones Mr. J. discovered one-hundred thirty-seven years later.

The diaries, written in a feminine hand, go into great detail about the activities, real and imagined, in which the man in black amused himself. According to the diaries, the room, situated in an isolated section of the second floor, was witness to hellish orgies and fiendish bloody rituals that involved debaucheries too chilling for the genteel feminine hand to record.

Mr. J. has seen this apparition only a few times. The appearance of the Captain is confined to the killing room - his former domicile. The present owner says that the Captain's appearances are always preceded by the smell of perique tobacco and the unmistakable stench of death.

Little did he realize, at the time, the continuing horror that remains in this room of pain. Through the years Mr. J. has owned a number of animals. At one time this included a Collie and a Doberman. Because of the degenerate character of the neighborhood, these animals were purchased for the security that only comes with large dogs. The hounds protected the property from would-be thieves for several years. One evening Mr. J. went out with friends. He secured his home. The dogs were left in the house, a not uncommon practice. Upon his return he was aware of a sullen silence pervading the old estate. He called his dogs. No response. He began to search for his beloved pets calling their names as he searched each room. On the second floor, in the killing room, he found them, or what was left of them. Both animals had been obscenely mutilated. His shock was enormous. He armed himself and began a painstaking, but futile, search of the premises. All the doors and windows were securely fashioned from the inside. There was no trace of the intruder. Mr. J. lovingly returned to his beloved animals. He tenderly gathered the grisly remains into a plastic bag. The next morning he brought the two dead animals to a veterinarian for an autopsy. It was revealed that the dogs had been dismembered with surgical precision. The wounds were straight and clean resembling the work of a surgeon's scalpel rather than a wild beast or a psychotic slasher. The most remarkable discovery of the autopsy was that the bodies had been completely drained of blood! The veterinarian could offer no explanation for his findings.

Mr. J. confessed to me that he noticed that the killing room was completely free of blood when he discovered his pets. The animals had been drained of their blood, but no trace of the crimson fluid could be found anywhere. It seemed as though the room has been, "licked clean" (Mr. J's terms). Shortly after this terrible incident, the violence spread. A cat was torn apart and apparently partially eaten. A second room harbored the remains of a stray dog. Panic overwhelmed the owner. Since no logical explanation could be formulated, he began to investigate these ghastly events through occult means. He sought the advice of Mr. Joe Culotta, a local radio personality and chemistry professor, who is also an active investigator of the bizarre and unusual. For several years, Mr. Culotta has held adult education classes at Tulane University that have delved into the supernatural. Mr. Culotta was able to introduce our besieged homeowner to several psychics and paranormal investigators - one of whom was the well-known Hans Holzer.

Mr. Holzer has written a number of works on ghosts, the occult and various paranormal phenomena. He also has been instrumental in solving several criminal cases through the use of psychometry. The powers and abilities of Mr. Holzer have been documented by police departments, newspapers, and a raft of objective, reliable witnesses. His credentials, as a bona fide psychic researcher, are unimpeachable. Mr. Holzer, accompanied by a medium with whom he works, conducted a series of investigations at the alleged haunted house. Their revelations were remarkable. Without any previous knowledge of the house's history, Mr. Holzer and his medium articulated a series of facts which were verified by the old diaries. They related the story of the diminutive governess and her deformed ward. They spoke of the unhallowed grave sequestered in an abandoned chimney. The images and events they related bore a chilling and uncanny resemblance to the facts of which Mr. J. was painfully aware. Mr. Holzer's conclusions bore witness to that which Mr. J. knew all along - the house is a center of highly charged psychic activity which has persisted for almost a century and a half.

Continuing along the lines of his occult investigations, Mr. J. sought the services of one Ms. Jane Alcott, a New Orleans personality and practicing white witch. Ms. Alcott instructed him in the procedure of a basic exorcism. She gave instructions to follow the procedure the next time he was confronted by spectral visitors. Mr. J. carried out her instructions and at first succeeded in quieting the ghosts for several months. However, as time passed, the visitations resumed. No subsequent exorcisms have had any effect. The ghosts remain and are active to this day.

While researching this story, this author was privy to several startling events which have left a lasting impression. During an interview with Mr. J. I became aware of a movement near a bookcase. I could not pin the movement down as a specific phenomenal event. I saw no human nor animal which could explain the movement. It was as though it was movement without anything being moved. This sounds crazy but there are no words to express what I sensed. During the course of the interview, my host excused himself momentarily. I took the opportunity to inspect the area around the bookcase and the bookcase itself. The area around the bookcase yielded no information out of the ordinary. The bookcase was an early nineteenth century rosewood masterpiece with ornate glass doors which were securely locked. I noticed brass bolts on the inside of each door which held them fast. Finding no evidence of any peculiarities, I returned to my seat. My host returned and we resumed the interview. Without warning the two locked bookcase doors, which I had only minutes before inspected, flew open with terrific force. I practically jumped through the ceiling. Mr. J. was absolutely non-pulsed by this unexpected occurrence. He laughed and said, "you see what I mean?"

I most certainly did. I must add that I inspected the two open doors and could discern no irregularities. The brass bolts were still extended from the locks which housed them. How more than an inch of solid brass on each lock could have become dislodged from their respective hooks without incurring damage to either lock or wood defies any explanation I can offer.

About one month later I returned to complete my interview and clear up a few hazy points. Our interview lasted approximately an hour. At its conclusion Mr. J. offered me a cocktail. I accepted. He left the room to prepare our refreshments. Several seconds later he returned. The poor man's face was flushed and his hands were trembling. In an unsteady voice he remarked, "my God, something awful has happened."

We walked into an adjacent room where a large bird cage stood in the north corner. I cautiously peered into the cage and faced a scene from hell. At the bottom of the locked cage were the remains of what was once a relatively large Cockatoo. The skull and vertebrae were intact, but without any flesh and virtually no trace of blood. Feathers were scattered pell-mell both in the cage and on the floor surrounding it. From all appearances the carnage appeared quite recent, within an hour or so. Quite frankly, I was too shocked to investigate the horror before my eyes any further. I might also add that Mr. J. was in no mood to continue the interview.

Reflecting on my experience I can only form two possible conclusions: (1) the house actually is besieged by malevolent forces of an unknown origin; (2) I had been the victim of a bizarre, actually insane, hoax. I have opted for the first conclusion for several reasons. I became aware of this house as haunted through a parapsychology class I attended at Tulane University.[3] Because of the fact the house had been the object of numerous scientific investigations by a number of competent individuals, all of these investigators shared the opinion that the house was a bona fide "haunted house." I, personally, had witnessed some unusual occurrences which totally mystified me. Finally, from my professional observations[4] of Mr. J. I could detect no dark psychotic blemish on his character which would impel such actions. He has no financial or affective stake in the reputation of the house as haunted. The man has lost several beloved pets. No, I can find no ulterior motive coming from this well-educated, sophisticated professional gentleman to explain the events of which I became aware.

As for the nature of the hauntings and blood thirsty assaults against the animals, I can formulate no adequate explanation. Suffice it to say that this mysterious old home has left impressions on me that I shall carry to my grave.

The Reverend's Wife

I n 1978 a young couple, Sandra and Pat Roberts, fulfilled part of a long held dream. They moved from the squeaky clean plastic suburbs into a fifty year-old house in an old mid-city neighborhood located on the outskirts of Bayou St. John. Their house was somewhat modern by their new neighborhood's standards. This split-level dwelling was constructed in the late 1920's while most of the other houses in the area dated to the turn of the century or before. The house wasn't as old as they would have liked, but it was ensconced in a neighborhood with Victorian homes and one-hundred plus year-old oaks.

Even before the purchase of their "new" home, Mrs. Roberts sensed something strange about this modest, stucco home. She was a real estate agent who had first-hand knowledge of the property's being put on the market. Desiring the house and the neighborhood, she and her husband went to see the house and speak with the owners, Mr. and Mrs. Holiday. The Holidays were selling the house because Mr. Holiday was terminally ill and wished to spend his remaining time in Florida with his physician sons. Upon arriving at the dwelling the young couple were ushered into a house draped with dark curtains hiding shuttered and barred windows. The inside of the pleasant looking house was dark and cave like. The denizens of this dark world were a pale couple who appeared aged beyond their years and two cats who, judging by the smell of the house, never ventured out of doors. The only illumination in the dark cavern was provided by small, incandescent fifteen watt lights. The old couple showed the Roberts around the house, but refused to discuss any possible sale or business because it was a Sunday, and their religious beliefs forbade the transaction of any business on the Sabbath. It was obvious that the Holidays were recluses and religious fanatics.[1]

The Roberts left a bit bemused at the eccentricity of the reclusive couple but were determined to return and conclude negotiations for the house they so much wanted. Within a few short weeks they were the proud owners of the house they so desired. Moving is always a hassle, and the Roberts' move was no exception. After a tiring day of crates, boxes and moving men, the happy couple was ready for their first night in their new home. No sooner had they retired than Mr. Roberts was awakened by the sound of footsteps climbing the stairs outside the couple's bedroom. He quickly jumped from his bed and proceeded to his dresser drawers in search of his .38 caliber revolver. A frantic search revealed no pistol even though it had been there earlier that morning. Greatly distressed and fearing for the safety of his family, Mr. Roberts armed himself with a club to confront the intruder who was now in the hall directly behind his bedroom door. He flung the door open, anticipating a pitched battle. His wife watched in terror. The hallway was empty. He searched the house. He awakened and questioned his two children. There was no explanation for the footfalls. The following morning Mr. Roberts conducted an exhaustive search in daylight hours, but still failed to surface the pistol.

These events and more continued night after night. Besides the footsteps, Pat and Sandra could hear a muffled voice whose words were indistinguishable. Pat armed himself with a shotgun and a club. Sleep became almost impossible for the hapless couple. This madness continued for almost two weeks. At this time, Mrs. Roberts met her next door neighbor, a Mrs. Genevieve Becker. In passing, Mrs. Becker commented that the Roberts must be night people as she was, because she noticed their lights burning all night long. It was at this point that Mrs. Roberts informed her of the strange occurrences in the house. After listening attentively, Mrs. Becker gave a knowing nod and said, "Oh, that must be the Reverend's wife."

Mrs. Becker explained that this stucco structure was once the abode of a Presbyterian minister and his spouse. The woman, who died in the house and for reasons unknown, still considered it her own. Mrs. Becker said the ghost was upset because the Roberts were strangers, interlopers who had invaded her world. The cure for this problem was simple - exorcism. Armed with water from Lourdes, a prayer and faith, Mrs. Becker was willing to go through the house room by room and introduce the Roberts to the former dead occupant of the Solomon Street property. Sandra Roberts was almost as amazed at this response as she was by the events that prompted this strange reply. She at first begged off, saying that she must consult her husband before agreeing to any ritual. Mrs. Becker was understanding, and encouraged her to counsel with her husband, Pat.

Feeling somewhat the fool, Sandra informed Pat of her strange conversation with Mrs. Becker. Her husband, sleepless for better than a dozen nights, was ready to agree with anything for some peace. He agreed. The next night the ritual was pronounced. The Roberts family, with their elderly exorcist, went from room to room sprinkling holy water, saying their prayers and being formally introduced to the Reverend's restless wife. After this simple ceremony, Mrs. Becker left. The Roberts, feeling a bit foolish, retired. Remarkably, the phenomenon ceased that very night. Mr. and Mrs. Roberts enjoyed an unremarkable restful night's repose, their first since taking possession of their new house. The ghost was silent. The following morning while Sandra was showering, her husband burst into the bathroom with a .38 revolver in his hand. "Why didn't you tell me you'd found the pistol?" he inquired.

Sandra, a bit startled by such a forceful entrance, replied, "Because I didn't find it. I thought it was still lost. Where was it?"

Pat told her that he found the pistol in his dresser drawer where it was always kept until its mysterious disappearance on the day they moved in. The gun appeared as mysteriously as it vanished. There was no chance of an oversight in the original search for the weapon. Pat had on several occasions searched not only the drawer where the pistol was kept, but all of the drawers in the dresser. In his efforts to surface his revolver, frustration had even forced him to empty the contents of each drawer and methodically pick through the contents. All of these actions availed him nothing. Then suddenly, the morning after the exorcism, the .38 appeared. Strange? That's not the word for it.

For the rest of their tenure in the house, the Roberts experienced absolutely no disturbances or unrest. Obviously the peculiar little ceremony worked. But here's the interesting aspect of the whole affair. Apparently, the manifestation, or ghost or whatever, was a reverent of the wife of a Presbyterian minister. I find it interesting that her ghost should be placated by holy water from Lourdes, a Catholic shrine. Also, the exorcism was orchestrated by a Catholic lay person, not a priest or religious. Could it be that the ghost was ecumenical in her belief? Or is it possible that spiritual comfort is unaware or unconcerned with the construct of religion, and only recognizes faith, ignoring the labels and bickerings of the human inventions of Catholicism or Presbyterianism, or whatever? An interesting question, but I'm afraid one without an answer.

After the Roberts left the house it had a succession of owners. None of them remained very long, and all seemed to experience an inordinate degree of bad luck. One, a young bachelor, was transferred to New Orleans with a promotion. He resided at the Solomon Street address for a little over two years. In that time he lost his job. He formed no lasting relationships, and finally he left. In leaving, he sold his house for over thirty thousand dollars less than he paid for it. His present whereabouts are unknown.

Then there was the young unmarried couple who took residence in the house for a scant eighteen months. They spoke constantly about something being wrong with their love nest. They were informed of the building's strange history by Mrs. Becker. Supposedly, they performed the same ritual as the Roberts. The results of their exorcism are unknown but their tenure was extremely brief for home owners.

So go the tales about a succession of owners. Today the attractive stucco home is owned by Barbara and Bruce Cramer and their young family. Mrs. Cramer stated that when she and her husband purchased this property, they had absolutely no knowledge of its haunted reputation. They did not learn of the alleged ghost until the day of their act of sale when their real estate agent informed them of the legends surrounding their new home. Mrs. Cramer said the agent treated the whole affair as a silly joke. I inquired if the Cramers had any experiences with this restless spirit? She replied that the house was absolutely normal. She had heard stories of the earlier exorcisms and remarked that they had probably worked. Whatever frightened the Roberts, and cast a pall of bad luck on subsequent owners, seems to be at rest - at least for now!

The Ghostly Mariner

An elderly man arrayed in seaman's garb haunts a residence at 1928 South Carrollton Avenue. He has been seen by dozens of people over the past several decades, and is impervious to exorcism. The first record of his existence dates from the early 1970's when renovation work was begun on the home.

Mr. James Blanchard, the owner of the house at the time, decided to construct an apartment in the basement to supplement his income. He hired a contractor and work was begun. When Mr. Blanchard returned home he found the workmen gone and virtually no work done on the planned apartment. In confusion he called the contractor for an explanation. The foreman told him that he could forget about any further work because none of his crew would ever set foot in that house again. No sooner had these sober, rugged men began work when they were confronted by a somber spectre drifting toward them on no earthly feet. Within seconds these burly men fled to their trucks and sped away. As can be imagined, the owner thought he had hired a group of moronic lunatics and sought a new, saner group of workers. The event repeated itself again and again.

Like most people, when faced with confusion and fear, the owner, a logical, hard boiled policeman, turned to religion. He contacted the Jesuit Fathers at Loyola University and explained his peculiar situation. After a certain degree of hesitancy the priests agreed to send one of their numbers to the haunted abode to perform an exorcism.[1] After much prayer, faith, and rivers of Holy Water the ghostly apparition was unaffected. The exorcism failed.

In the story, "The Reverend's Restless Wife," another exorcism was cited which was successful. The question naturally arises why one exorcism performed by a Catholic lay woman against a Protestant ghost should succeed while another exorcism officiated by a Catholic priest should fail. I believe that the common denominator in both instances is faith. Not the faith of the living, but the faith of the dead. The Reverend's wife had faith in the Christian concept of God. This faith quieted her haunting and settled her soul. Now this is only conjecture, but it does seem to fit a theory which I'll explain. Possibly, the ancient mariner was without faith, ergo, the exorcism, based on faith had no effect upon him.

If ghosts are real, and a large body of evidence points at some reality beyond the grave, then it seems that the beliefs of the dead or at least some vestige of their beliefs also exists in that world of darkness, silence and secrecy. Then what does this say about faith itself and the basis of faith, i.e., God? Perhaps that which can be inferred by this theory is that truth is a totally subjective phenomenon. If one holds to the opinion of God and Satan and such, then these beliefs are real and tangible to the subject even past death. Conversely, if these tenets of beliefs are negated by the subject then these tenets cease to be real and exhibit no control over his/her activities either in life or death. Whether this theory will one day evolve into law, who can say; however, it does offer a possible explanation as to the success of some exorcisms and the abysmal failure of others.

Let's get back to our roving mariner. After the efforts of almost a dozen work crews the renovations were finally completed. The pragmatic policeman decided to sell his improved property and reap the financial fruits of his labor and planning. He found a buyer, a Dr. Denshins and his family. The ghost remained with the property. Footsteps were heard. Objects moved. All without cause. Seemingly, the ghost presented no special problem for the Denshins, for they apparently accepted it with a certain degree of bemusement.

Again the house changed hands. Ms. Adrian McCranie and her family became the next owners. I spoke at length with Ms. McCranie via a telephone interview. Basically, she related witnessing the same occurrences as the previous occupants. However, she added an important subjective viewpoint that I feel is valid to consider. Ms. McCranie said that great courage was never one of her strong points. In fact she described herself as, ". . . a real scardy cat . . ." Nevertheless, she said she never felt scared or threatened when confronted by whatever it was that she would sometimes sense. She felt that the presence, which was always enveloped in a mist, was benevolent. Occasionally, articles of clothing or personal effects would disappear, but would always return. In fact, most of the individuals interviewed in the course of this research have voiced similar opinions. By and large, the majority of human encounters with the ghosts (or whatever) are usually without malevolent overtones. Very little literature on hauntings and ghosts account violence or evil.

Why is it then that we associate these denizens of the unknown with vile deeds and monstrous acts? I believe the explanation is simple enough. We are afraid of the unknown. This fear forces us, as humans, to project the unknown evils within ourselves onto the external unknowns of the world and give them that repressed evil face that lurks within each of us. Basically speaking, ghosts are much maligned, not for their actions but from our fear of the demons within our own hearts and souls. I might also add that these demons are our own creations.

The Undead Comrades

T he War Between the States left a trail of bloody pages in America's history. It also left a legacy of ghosts and hauntings throughout the South. The tragic story of Captain Hugh Devers and Quartermaster Charles Cromley is part of that legacy.

By 1 May 1862, New Orleans was firmly in the hands of the Union Army. Martial law was declared. Private property was seized to garrison and support the invading army. One such hapless piece of real estate was the stately mansion that concerns our present inquiry. The records do not indicate who the residents were during that dark spring of '62; however, they do indicate what the Union troops discovered in the appropriated property. The soldiers invaded the house and began searching for valuables, contraband and any remnant of the shattered Confederate forces. In a third floor room the battle hardened troops were confronted with a ghastly sight of horror and mayhem. Chained to the walls, either dead or dying, were about a dozen slaves.[1] The poor wretches had been brutally tortured and then left to die in the abandoned house. The dead were buried. The others were hospitalized. A detachment of men cleaned and refurbished the house.

As soon as the property was restored, Devers and Cromley were billeted in the elegant residence. They brought their fashionable Bostonian wives to their commandeered mansion. The two couples proceeded to immerse themselves in the social life of an ancient city turned to spoils. There were balls and masques. Sumptuous dinners and dazzling socials were all part of the officers' lives. They lived well. They lived as conquerors.

Part of their grand lifestyle was the gambling houses on Rue Royale. These occasions of gaming were the beginning of their tragic demise. Running low on funds and burdened by escalating debts, those two officers devised a plan which, if successful, would end all of their financial difficulties. Devers and Cromley decided to fake a robbery of the Union payroll which was under their care each month. Their plan succeeded. The money was theirs. The only problem was that their superior, General Benjamin Butler, smelled a rat. Butler launched a full scale investigation which grew to indictable proportions.

Devers and Cromley, trained officers as they were, soon saw the hopelessness and disgrace of their eventual court martials and subsequent executions. Both men being gentlemen, albeit, theives, elected upon their only honorable escape - mutual suicide.[2]

Several nights later a gala ball was planned by a Union colonel. It was on this night of festivity that these two officers planned their deaths. Both men dressed in their smartest uniforms. They polished their boots and their brass. They buckled on their heavy sabres and colorful campaign ribbons. These two who were about to die were resplendent in their military regalia. In their need to buy time and insure the privacy needed for their desperate act, they sent their wives before them to the home of some friends, the Fenlons. They excused themselves on account of military business. If their delay was longer than anticipated, they instructed their wives to attend the ball with the Fenlons.[3]

Insured of their privacy, the two soon-to-be-disgraced officers mounted the stairs to their cramped rooms on the third floor.
In this room which once held chained and mutilated slaves the
two comrades in arms and theft gave one another one last
inspection and farewell. Both men lay side by side on a thin
mattress. They unholstered their .44 caliber Colt revolvers,
pressed them to each others' hearts, and simultaneously pulled
the triggers.

Later that morning their corpses were found side by side on
that blood soaked mattress. The amount of blood was so
profuse that the crimson lake had seeped through the floor
boards to the room below. So should have ended a sad story
of greed and dishonor. But It didn't. What became of the
purloined Union payroll? Had it been squandered on gambling
and raucous living? Or had the stolen cache been sequestered
in some unknown vault? The truth was known only to the two
dead officers.

Eventually, the house was converted for commercial purposes. In turn the old house became a factory for perfumes,
then lamps and finally mattresses.[4] All during these various
occupancies strange events and rumors persisted about the
tragic house. Occupants heard the cadence of heavy boots
coming from the third floor. Loud singing of patriotic songs was
heard. When these events were investigated, no explanation
could be offered for the strange activities which so beleaguered
this edifice of shame and remorse. Apart from the singing and
thundering boots many passersby reported the pale countenance of two Union troops glaring from the upstairs windows.
The stories persisted. Finally, one Isadore Seelig took possession of the property. While renovating the structure, Mr. Seelig
was almost crushed by a gigantic concrete block which virtually flew down the stairs. Seelig ran upstairs to investigate the
near fatal mishap. All of the upstairs windows and doors were

bolted from the inside. Stranger still, he found no scratches or grit from the huge block which slammed down the steps. There was absolutely no evidence as to the origin of the potentially lethal chunk of concrete.[5]

During the 1930's the haunted mansion became a rooming house. A widow occupied rooms directly below that accursed third floor. Soon after moving in, the widow was peering through her window. She felt something moist dripping on her arm. Her arm was covered by a growing red stain. She looked up and saw the ceiling saturated with blood. The next day she vacated the premises.[6]

The house retained its eerie reputation. No tenant would occupy it. Neighbors crossed the street to avoid its malevolent presence. Finally, in the 1970's, a young couple purchased the house with the intent of restoring it to its former opulence. This couple, Kathleen and Anthony Jones, reported in a 1977 interview that they had experienced no hauntings or paranormal activity,[7] however, for whatever reason, the house was never occupied.

An interesting sidelight to this house of mysteries occurred in August 1951 when a hurricane demolished the slave quarters in the back yard. As the debris was being cleared, a tunnel was discovered under the house. The tunnel led to the street and dead ended. Several old trunks containing uniforms, chains, and rubbish were unearthed, but no hint of any treasure was surfaced. No one knew the purpose of the tunnel, nor who built it. It has remained unexplained to this day.

Let us return to the present. While researching this site, I attempted to interview several residents of this old, decaying neighborhood. Most would not speak with me; however, one old black man who asked to remain anonymous related a bizarre tale about the old mansion.

He told me that during the late seventies any deserted house in the area (which is near the Saint Thomas Housing Project) became fair game for dope addicts. The old gentleman said that was the fate of our haunted house. Within a month the hop heads deserted the house because they saw two white men "in police uniforms" who routinely interrupted their revelries by walking through walls and singing, "old timey songs," with drawn revolvers and the look of death on their faces.

Today, the house is occupied by local sculptor, Norman Therrien, Lynn, his wife and their eleven year-old son, Alexander. I contacted Mrs. Therrien via telephone. She said her family was aware of the haunted reputation of their old home, but they had never witnessed any strange manifestations. Evidently, Devers and Cromley have finally found peace.

The Deadly Dentist

Searching for this pair of ghosts might provide a delightful culinary, if not mystic, experience. In the 1850's the Coffee Pot Restaurant was the office of the strange dentist, Dr. Xavier Deschamps. Dr. Deschamps was a large, muscular man of frightening countenance. His huge body was covered with coarse hair giving him a simian rather than human appearance.[1] Being a dentist he was an educated man with a knowledge of medicine and science. Anesthetics were finding their place in the world of medicine and Dr. Deschamps, ever the modern pioneer, experimented with their use. Chloroform, nitrous oxide, opiates and other such drugs were investigated by him. He was also interested in hypnotism, and practiced it in the pursuit of his profession. Today, drugs and hypnotism are necessary and respected methods of medical treatment. It was through the researches of these early scientists that human misery has been greatly reduced, and the quality of human life dramatically improved.

However, there was another side to this respected dentist and man of science. He was interested in that peculiarly American phenomenon of the mid-nineteenth century - spiritualism. The good doctor engaged in seances, and attempts to communicate with the dead. His dabblings in these occult practices were not confined to scientific curiosity alone. He had baser ambitions for these esoteric experiments - the discovery of hidden treasure.[2] It was toward this end that he became a precursor of that modern fiend, Charles Manson. As a dentist, he had plenty of opportunity to meet and influence substantial numbers of young women. With his knowledge of drugs and hypnotism combined with an aggressive, powerful personality, he had his way with numerous young ladies who lost all resistance to his vices.

He soon became convinced that one of his patients had powerful mediumistic abilities. Plying her with drugs and hypnotic suggestions, he began using her in his seances in the hope of discovering treasure. His seances were continual failures. For this he blamed his sweet, innocent victim. Each failure was accompanied by brutal physical and sexual assaults. The unfortunate girl had fallen under his spell. She could not escape or perhaps did not wish to escape. No matter, the seances continued. So did their failure. So did the violent, sadistic assaults. Finally, after months of drug and physical abuse, the poor girl died. The "Mad Doctor" was promptly arrested, charged, tried and executed for the girl's murder.[3] This should be the end of a shocking crime which today has become something unfortunately common; however, that was not the case. For well over a century people have reported sightings of the monstrous, leering doctor re-enacting his vile, passionate crime upon his helpless, cringing victim.

A heinous crime enacted time and time again is the basis of many ghost stories. The perpetrator and his victim are doomed to repeat the deed over and over, with little, if any, variation. In a sense, it is almost like a film or recording played again and again and again. Strong emotions and violence are theorized to leave a kind of imprint on the environment where they transpired. A catalyst such as the anniversary of the tragic event or certain meteorological conditions or some unknown factors trigger a re-enactment of the event. Ghosts of this nature are highly predictable - it's similar to watching reruns. They seldom, if ever, interact with the living who witness their torment.

It was this type of ghost that the old sources described, interesting, but not very dynamic.[4] In order to surface more recent accounts of these stories, the author attempts, whenever possible, to interview present day inhabitants of the old haunts. In this instance, because it is a place of business, there are no occupants to question. Instead, I spoke with the employees of this charming cafe.

I introduced myself, and explained my mission to the manager, Randy Barber. He listened attentively, smiled and then told me that I should speak with two employees, Louise Johnson and Pearl Jefferson. These two cooperative ladies had been employed at this establishment for a total of 57 years, and in that time had gathered a collection of astounding anecdotes. The ghost with whom they were most familiar was feminine: Dr. Deschamps' victim, I would assume. More interestingly, this female spirit was dynamic and highly interactive. She is responsible for numerous and continuing poltergeist activity. For years pots and pans, plates and flatware have mysteriously been transported about the cafe moved by no earthly hands. Objects of all sorts have mysteriously vanished only to reappear just as mysteriously. These occurrences are so common that both women expect them as almost daily happenings. The strangest part of this haunting is that this ghost not only transports objects, but actually communicates vocally. Each woman recounted stories where she could hear a woman's voice calling her name. This seems to indicate that this presence is actually aware of its environment and that environment's present occupants. The source of the voice is usually unseen; however, on occasion a shade or shadow is detected. Beside verbal communication our unrested spirit will sometimes place an ethereal hand on the bodies of various living workers. Louise Johnson said that this can be a somewhat unnerving experience to which one never becomes quite accustomed.

Finally, there is the story of a huge black cat who, no matter how secure the kitchen, seems to gain entrance at will. Try as one might, nobody has ever been able to catch or coax the dark feline. A cat in a kitchen might not seem too strange, but this cat has been on the scene for more than thirty years!

Each woman seemed quite sincere in relating her respective experiences to me. These employees are honest, hard working individuals who would have no reason to come out of the kitchen and spin tall tales for the amusement of one, somewhat, eccentric writer. What would they gain? Also, their accounts were too matter-of-fact to have been rehearsed. The restaurant does not build its advertising around ghosts or hauntings so any commercial predicate of this nature is without validity. My opinion is that these bizarre tales are the product of actual experience.

After my interview with these ladies I spoke with several other employees who all were of the same opinion - something strange is manifest in the cafe.

Penelope

n 1832 Dr. Joseph A. Tricou built a classic French Quarter domicile. The gorgeous home is important to us because it houses the very active ghost of his grand niece Penelope Tricou who was the victim of an accident which claimed her life in 1874. Hapless Penelope lost her footing on the third floor stairs and tumbled to her death with a broken neck. Penelope's tragedy so affected the elderly physician that he sold his home shortly after the fatal mishap. As fate would have it, Penelope's demise was not the end of her activities in the Bourbon Street mansion.[1]

Interestingly enough, this author became aware of Penelope through a conversation with a young lady of his acquaintance, Ms. Daphne Lee. I mentioned my project, *New Orleans Ghosts*. I related several stories. She listened to my tales with interest. Then she asked me what I knew about Penelope. Despite my extensive efforts to find and record the Crescent City's ghosts, I had to confess my ignorance. She then related the following story which impelled the investigation which resulted in this story.

In the beginning of June 1990, Ms. Lee sought employment at the Tricou House which is now a restaurant featuring authentic Creole cuisine and live jazz entertainment. She was successful in her quest for employment. While sitting in the upstairs business office filling out her tax forms the lights began to blink off and on. The manager, Calvin Sinclaire, noticing Ms. Lee's surprise, told her that the flickering lights were Penelope's way of telling Ms. Lee hello and welcome. He then went on to explain Penelope's status as the resident ghost and a few anecdotes about her antics.

After hearing this story I concluded that it merited an investigation and possible inclusion in, *New Orleans Ghosts.* Friday, 22 June 1990 I entered the Tricou house and requested an interview with the manager. I explained my purpose and the manager suggested that I speak with one Mr. Bruce Averell who had been employed at the Tricou House for about eight years as a general maintenance engineer.

Mr. Averell presented himself as a practical, level-headed young man. He is a responsible worker who is both alert and intelligent. His faculties as a witness seem quite valid which adds credence to the tale he related. Mr. Averell reported that during his tenure at the Tricou House he personally has heard the sounds of footsteps walking right up to him when no one was there. He estimated that he has encountered this phenomenon literally hundreds of times. Apart from this acoustical manifestation, Mr. Averell reported, as did Ms. Lee, electrical disturbances which caused lights to flicker, in some instances to burn out all together. Try as he may, he has yet to be able to either correct or trace the cause of this electrical annoyance.

All of this is interesting enough, but the story which most captured my imagination had to do with a near fatal mishap. One morning several workmen under the supervision of Mr. Averell were repairing the ceiling of a second story veranda. Suddenly, a man screamed. All eyes fired toward the scream to see one of the carpenters careening backwards from the porch's railing. In an instant his fall was interrupted and he was hurled back to safety. Upon inquiry, the man reported that he was grabbed by someone and pushed powerfully from the almost certain death that awaited him on the solid concrete twenty plus feet below. The event was absolutely without rational explanation.[2] It is here that I wish to add a personal observation. Several times during Mr. Averell's narrative I noticed the appearance of "goose bumps" on the flesh of his arms. He himself even commented that, "when I think about the accident, I get chills."

If this story is true, then an inference can be made about so-called ghosts in general and Penelope specifically. From my investigations, I have heard stories of ghosts that sound like stories of living persons. Some are mischievous, even evil. Others are concerned about human welfare and act to avert tragedy. This affective interaction leads me to believe that whatever spiritual manifestations may be, a certain category of them are governed by individual personalities much like our own. If ghosts really are representatives of some type of existence beyond the grave, then they seemingly retain certain vestiges of what they were in their physical lives. If, in fact, the workman's life was spared by Penelope, this leads me to believe that she acted out of concern for a fellow human who would have shared her unfortunate fate had she not intervened. Further speculation is unwarranted except to say that the qualities of the human experience may possibly transcend death and validate the integrity of the self above and apart from the illusions of time and matter that we hold to be so self-evident.

El Viejo Garrison de España

During the bygone day of the Spanish occupation of New Orleans (1762-1800) an alleged mutiny and theft gave birth to a terror-filled legend that persists to this day. A blood thirsty group of Spanish soldiers, lusting for the gold and precious gems safeguarded in their garrison, mutinied against their officers and fellow soldiers. The victims of this treason were brutally tortured. The unfortunates were stripped naked. Meat hooks were dug into their flesh in order to suspend them from a wall. Long iron spikes were then driven through their feet and legs in order to arrest their thrashing and keep them still for even more ghastly attentions.

The mutineers captured a number of large river rats which they fastened around the waists of some of the loyal troops. Rats in place, iron kettles were tied over the bound rats. The kettles were then heated with open flames forcing the rats to gnaw through the men's bellies to seek refuge in their intestines. Others were subjected to equally monstrous tortures and humiliations. When the sadistic orgy was spent, the broken, bloodied bodies, some still clinging desperately to life, were sequestered with mortar and brick in the very wall which had supported their agony. The scoundrels evaporated into the night, some to disappear forever, others to found rich and powerful families financed by a treasure bathed in blood and abomination. These acts of insane terror and brutality allegedly did not end on that dreadful date. It is said that this obscene event spawned a company of ghosts who still haunt the site of that ancient tragedy. Unsuspecting tenants of the great, square building have given frightening accounts of encounters with legions of eviscerated and hideously mutilated men. Reports of giant, man eating, spectral rats have been voiced by renters who escaped with their lives to warn their neighbors of the terror that waited behind the thick, somber walls which border Burgundy and Barracks Streets. For better than a century tales of perverse terror have drifted from the matrix of evil that locals refer to as the old Spanish garrison.

In 1932 a group of young men were allowed   rent-free lodgings in the morose old barracks. Since it was the height of the Great Depression, and they were down on their luck, they accepted readily. At first everything seemed normal enough. Then, one sullen night, one of the guys noticed a light coming from a room at the top of the garret staircase. He could also see what appeared to be a man counting gold coins. Perplexed, he ascended the twisting stairs. Where he had spied the solitary figure there was nothing but a solid stone wall. He descended to the courtyard, looked up, and again saw the mysterious form. Quickly, he summoned his two friends. Armed with flashlights and tape measures, they tried to pin down the elusive tenant.   All of their efforts were in vain.

A short time later, during an explosive thunderstorm, two of our beleaguered guests were accosted by a troop of zombie-like soldiers who appeared to walk out of the wall. They were

confronted by a parade of men stumbling toward them with trailing intestines and empty eye sockets. Hanging on the wall from which the zombies stalked were other wretched figures being devoured in grim agony by huge carnivorous rats. Blood washed down those cursed walls as screams tore out of tongueless mouths. Enough is enough. The nauseating spectacle proved too much for the young gentlemen's constitutions to endure. Our once happy trio fled into the night never again to return.

The alleged history and haunting of this great, grey edifice seem to be the classic ingredients of which ghosts and paranormal phenomena are made. There is only one problem with the old Spanish garrison. It was not constructed until 1830, some 30 years after Spanish rule ended in Louisiana. The story is a hoax that has been kept alive in oral tradition for more than a century and is recorded as gospel in at least one source.

The old Spanish garrison is included in this collection because it is a part of the city's supernatural folklore. A story about greed and mutilation and murder strikes a dark, responsive cord in our psyches. If such stories also include a ghost, so much the better. We give this ghost a "life" so to speak, by relating stories about it and even individualizing and embellishing those stories, which, in a sense, communicates to our listeners something about us as individuals. The old Spanish garrison is indeed a New Orleans ghost because it speaks to us of the spirit of fear and horror that is in all of us.

Pere Dagobert

I t has long been rumored in the Crescent City that during
bleak rain swept nights in the hours before dawn a sweet
tenor voice can be heard singing the "Kyrie." The song drifts
through the dripping air between St. Louis Cathedral and the St.
Louis Cemetery. It is only a voice. There is no accompanying
apparition.[1]

The owner of this voice was a charming Capuchin priest,
Pere Dagobert. Pere Dagobert arrived in New Orleans in 1745
to become pastor of the Church of Saint Louis, what is now St.
Louis Cathedral. He was an exceedingly popular priest who
exhibited that French, joie de vivre. Pere Dagobert was a
handsome, cultured and urban French gentleman, as well as a
priest. He had a love of good food, good wine and the good life.
His temperament and manners fit perfectly with the growing
new world city of New Orleans. Pere Dagobert led his French
flock and was loved by them. He was more than a priest. He
nursed the sick and counseled the desperate. He became the
benefactor of widows and orphans. He welcomed the new
born and buried the dead. Such was the life of this somewhat
worldly but godly man.

Suddenly, in October 1764 Jean Jacques-Blaise Dabbadie, acting governor of Louisiana, announced to the French colonists of New Orleans that by act of the Treaty of Fountainebleau they were now subjects of the Spanish crown. Chaos erupted. The proud French families of New Orleans organized support from the surrounding area and formally petitioned Louis XV not to cede New Orleans to Spain. The petition failed, but that failure sowed the seeds of what some considered the new world's first open rebellion for independence.[2]

5 March 1766 arrived and with it the new Spanish governor, Don Antonio de Ulloa, a respected scientist, scholar and naval officer. He was instantly hated. Almost as immediately, a plot was hatched to free New Orleans from Spanish "tyranny." The insurrection was led by the wealthiest and most powerful of

New Orleans' aristocracy. These men were also part of Pere Dagobert's flock. The insurrection was a success. On 1 November 1768 the governor exited to Havana and safety. This "independence," actually anarchy, lasted until 16 August 1769.[3] On that date, Don Alejandro O'Reilly, an Irish expatriate, arrived in New Orleans. The 3,190 men, women, children and slaves were awakened by a fully armed Spanish fleet of twenty-four ships bearing 2,000 plus marines. The "rebellion" folded and the leaders were arrested. On 24 October 1769 five rebel leaders were shot to death by firing squad: Lafreniere, Noyan, Caresse, Marquis and Joseph Milhet. A sixth, Joseph Villere, was bayoneted during a scuffle and later died awaiting trial.[4] It is here that the ghostly tradition begins. O'Reilly refused to bury the men. He allowed the six corpses to fester in the rain and heat. The shock was unbelievable. How could a Catholic - even an Irish expatriate Catholic - refuse a decent Catholic burial to those with whom he shared brotherhood in Christ? It was an atrocity, but what could possibly be done under the watchful eye of a Spanish garrison directed by a blood-thirsty Irishman?

Pere Dagobert had the answer: In the stillness of the night he gathered the families of the six fallen patriots at the Church of St. Louis. There to the amazement of the families lay the bodies of their fallen fathers, husbands and sons. Pere Dagobert, with assistance of Pere Etienne and Pere Hypolite, sang the funeral mass. After mass, in a driving rainstorm, the funeral procession proceeded to St. Louis Cemetery No. 1 where the bodies were properly interred with all of the offices of the Church.[5] This miracle was never forgotten by the city's French. The story has become part of myth, and perhaps it is that myth's voice that we may hear in the early morning rain storms that occasionally shroud the French Quarter?

Beauregard-Keyes House

The Beauregard-Keyes House is a designated National Historic Place. During the day its antique laden rooms host throngs of tourists who come to visit the one-time residence of the Confederate's Napoleon in Gray in Gen. Pierre Gustave Toutant Beauregard (1818-1893). The home is a cheerful, airy, historic enjoyment for those fortunate enough to be guided through its spacious interior by attractive knowledgeable guides dressed in colorful period costumes. But, rumors have circulated about a dark side to the grand old mansion.

There are those who say that after the tourists and guides have left for the day the house experiences a weird, unearthly transformation. The entire interior seems to fade into another time. The furniture and accoutrements melt into another dimension. A pervasive darkness descends on the rooms transforming them into a world of shadows and shifting shapes. Suddenly, the rooms burst to life with scenes conjured from hell. Men with mangled limbs and blown-away faces swirl in a confused dance of death. Horses and mules appear and are slaughtered by grapeshot and cannon. The pungent smell of blood and decay permeates the restless atmosphere. All around is the mindless violence of the battlefield. The ghostly spectacle is a moving panorama of the carnage and death of war. Abruptly, from the maelstrom brewing in the elegant rooms, a diminutive figure appears clad in a Confederate general's gray and gold uniform. As the spectre of the old soldier moves through the phantom battlefield he can be heard to groan one word, "Shiloh."[1]

In order to understand the nature of this alleged haunting it is necessary to know some of the facts concerning General Beauregard's life. The facts that concern us have to do with the role he played in that great American tragedy - the Civil War. The first shots that began the Civil War were fired upon Fort Sumpter 12 April 1861 at the order of the Creole general.[2] This act initiated a conflict that would consume the lives of over one-half million American citizens.

During the ensuing war years Beauregard performed with skill, courage and effectiveness. He was a dashing cavalry officer who was partly responsible for the stunning Confederate victory at Bull Run. It was here that almost 15,000 men lost their lives,[3] and the Union almost lost the will to pursue the war.

Almost a year to the day (6-7 April 1862) after Beauregard fired those fateful shots against Fort Sumpter, the Battle of Shiloh raged. Confederate generals Johnson and Beauregard squared off against Union generals Grant and Buell. When the smoke cleared and the dust settled, approximately 25,000 men lay dead and the Confederate army was in full retreat. Eventually, the war ended and Beauregard returned to New Orleans. Part of his time in the Crescent City was spent at his home which would later be called the Beauregard-Keyes House. Beauregard wrote books and dwelled upon the great American tragedy that began with his order to fire upon Fort Sumpter. His actions changed the course of American history as dramatically as the Revolutionary War. It also began a conflict that left more Americans dead than all of the wars America has ever fought combined. Perhaps it was the force of this knowledge which

somehow projected itself through the "Napoleon in Gray" into the environment in which he once brooded and reflected?

Nevertheless, The Beauregard-Keyes house is remarkable for it also is the alleged home of another "family" of ghosts.

If the old legends and tales are to be believed, the building is a virtual ghost dormitory. In addition to the old Confederate General and his battle it was also the scene of a bloody shoot out whose violence still clings to the ancient walls. It has been reported that after the sun has set and the cares of the day slip into the velvety night, four dark, swarthy figures can be seen stealthily moving along the upper side and rear galleries. The men are armed. They move with a purpose motivated by greed, vengeance and murder. They creep with their backs to the wall, eyes gleaming with a blood red nimbus in the dim light.

Suddenly, the silence is shattered by the loud report of powerful handguns. The dark figures fire back. Ghostly lead rends and rips ghostly flesh. Spectral bones are splintered and shattered. Blood spews against the pastel walls. Streams of crimson gush from open wounds to pour into the yard below.

One, then two, then three men fall dead from the lethal exchange of shot. A fourth assassin, critically wounded, descends from the balcony on unseen wings. His face is the screaming mask of a rotting corpse. Once on the ground he and his screams disappear into the vaporous darkness. Abruptly, all again is silence. The gallery, which but seconds before held the horror of death and mutilation, is without trace of blood or bodies. The ghosts have vanished.[4]

The phantom gun fight traces its origin to the 1890's. During the turn of the nineteenth century, New Orleans experienced a wave of immigration by Sicilians. The majority of these new arrivals were poor, but hard-working, good people. Unfortunately, among the good were also the evil. This time period saw the growth of several Sicilian crime organizations such as the Black Hand and the Mafia. These organizations were powerful, ruthless and fearless. It is alleged that certain Mafia members were responsible for the brutal shotgun assassination of New Orleans police superintendent David C. Hennessy.[5] Extortion, murder and kidnapping were the stock in trade of these thugs.

It came as no surprise that the family of Corrado Giacona, a wealthy Sicilian wine merchant, should fall under the baleful eye of the Mafia. Giacona and his family were threatened with violence unless they paid $5,000 in protection money. Evidently Mr. Giacona was not the type of man to knuckle under. He turned the old Beauregard mansion into a fortress. He barred the windows. He installed heavy, bolted doors. More importantly, he armed himself and his family with large caliber revolvers, and made sure they knew how to use them. Finally after months of fear, the Mafia decided to make their move. One night in 1909 as the Giacona family enjoyed their evening meal, in the privacy of their fortress, four cutthroats tried to gain entrance through an upstairs gallery. The alert Giaconas gave an armed response. After a pitched gun battle which splintered doors and shattered glass, three of the Mafiosi lay dead of multiple gunshot wounds. The fourth, critically wounded, escaped through a curtain of hot lead and even hotter Latin tempers.[6] The Giaconas lived in relative peace until the early 1920's. Finally, the family moved and disappeared from history. The house was converted to a macaroni factory in 1925. At this time many New Orleanians interested in preserving the historic structure formed the Beauregard Memorial Association. During those years before World War II strange stories began to circulate about the property. Reports surfaced of neighbors and passersby hearing the din of battle. Sabers were heard to clash. Men screamed and cursed. Musket fire shattered the still, humid air. Others saw the blasted, bleeding bodies of Mafiosi toughs dripping blood from the upstairs gallery. Some saw blazing revolvers spewing fire and lead, but held by no earthly hands.

It is worthwhile to note these hauntings took a long time to become manifest. Certainly, strange and powerful emotions were associated with each individual who allegedly left a spectral signature on this grand house, but why did so much time pass between the various events and the paranormal phenomena? What was the catalyst that prompted these events to occur? This is a question with no answer.

The director of the Beauregard House, Alma H. Neal, said in a 1977 interview, "We do not know anything supernatural taking place here . . ."[7] In researching this story I enquired of a tour guide about the hauntings. She shrugged off my enquiry and said that ". . . all that talk of spectres and ghosts is just so many old wives' tales."

The alleged ghosts follow a deterministic pattern. They don't seem to interact with humans who claim to see them. All of them surround figures who obviously experienced great emotional stress; however, their existence is denied by those who should know. Are these ghosts real? Does a conspiracy of silence enshroud the truth? Those who can answer these questions probably never will.

The Octoroon Mistress

F inding this enchanting New Orleans ghost might be hazardous to one's health. It is not because she's a blood thirsty harpy from hell bent only on human destruction. Nor is she a succubus intent on sucking the life from the foolish. Her danger lies in the fact that she is a seasonal apparition who only appears on the roof of her abode during the coldest and stormiest of nights of December. Her beautiful, sepia, naked body can only be seen from the hours of midnight to dawn on the most inclement December nights. As with the majority of ghosts, she is very predictable. She is locked into a specific time frame, and her activities are unvarying. She appears only on the worst of December nights and simply paces carefully across the slippery slate roof. After a night of endless pacing she fades into the roof with the first rays of dawn.

It should be mentioned that although her activities are the classic predictable activities displayed by the majority of ghosts she does display a certain individuality. She always appears naked. Very few ghosts are so immodest.[1]

The mulatto mistress' story begins in the brutal days of slavery. Her name was Julie and she was beautiful. She, as her race, was the captive of the "peculiar institution," as slavery was called by Ante-bellum aristocrats. One of the less discussed aspects of slavery was the eugenic experiments which resulted in human beings being called mulatto (1/2 black), quadroon (1/4 black), and octoroon (1/8 black). The process went something like this - An attractive Negro woman would become the mistress of, or more likely, be raped by her master. If the result of such a union was a girl - lighter than her mother - the process would be repeated. The results of these unions between healthy, attractive black females and strong, virile "aristocrats" of European descent resulted in an infamous history expressed by the quadroon balls and reflected in city ordinances.[2] Such women were prized for their exotic beauty, cultured ways and surging passion.

Such a woman was Julie. Her rich, French master was also her ardent lover. He dressed her coffee au lait body in silks and brocades. She had her own room with a toilet kept by "her" slaves. Nightly she indulged in the finest roast meats and delicacies from the Gulf and lake.[3] Heady wine and ecstatic sex ended her nights. Her life was one of ease and pleasure except for the occasional abortion which terrified her and wracked her with pain.

Yet she was unhappy. Though she lived as a queen it was in a gilded cage. Whenever her master, her lover, entertained, she would be locked in her rooms and forgotten. She wanted their love to be open for the world to see. After all, she was 7/8 white, spoke fluent French and Spanish, and had the looks that could confuse even the most practiced eyes. Why should he not marry her? Such a practice, though seldom discussed, had an established precedent. For days on end she begged, reasoned, pled for a promise of betrothal. She loved him. She wanted to be one with him for all time in the eyes of God and men. Marriage, to bear his children, to show the power of their love to the world was her only desire.

Her master reacted at first with amusement. He loved her more because of her love for him. Their ecstatic sex reached new heights fueled by the madness of the fantasy. When the master's passion faded into the satin sheets with his sweat, so did the fantasy. The idea of actually, legally, marrying a woman of color was unthinkable. His family and friends would shun him. Society would cease to respect him. The entire idea was perverted. His resolve to end the fantasy was only met by greater persistence by Julie. Soon his amusement turned to ridicule, then to blows. Still the lovely Julie begged. His sex life fell to ruin. His domestic haven had become a house of anxiety. At his wits end, he formulated a compromise. He entered Julie's bedroom. The forlorn Julie sat heartbroken on the beautiful bed that had once been their world, their love. Her master said he would marry her if she would prove her love for him. Her heart zoomed with hope and joy. Yes, of course, she would do anything to prove her love for him . . . anything.

The conditions of her proof were that she should retire to the roof on that very cold, stormy December and remain until dawn - absolutely nude. The master was confident that his request would go unanswered and he could again settle into the domestic and sexual bliss to which he was accustomed.

Julie's love and determination were equal to the task. She accepted the challenge. Her master watched in amazement as she mounted the tiny stairs that led to the roof. The cold rain pelted her soft, tan skin like bullets. The wind lashed her thick, dark hair into her face and eyes. She fought against the razor tongues of wind that licked at her balance on the slippery tiles. She endured the pain. She endured the horror. Tomorrow she would be his wife - for this she would endure hell!

As the master smugly awaited her return, a guest arrived. Someone with whom he could forget this madness. They smoked. They drank absinthe and cognac. They played chess and entertained one another until dawn. The affair with Julie was aborted from his mind for hours. He knew that he would return to her room and find her warm, sleeping, naked and beautiful. No more marriage foolishness.

The room was deserted. He ran to the tiny stairs and onto the roof. It was there huddled near the eave of the roof that he saw the crumpled, frozen form of his beautiful Julie.[4]

There is evidence of a second haunting concerning this house. Some have reported seeing, reflected in some of the windows, the figure of a lonely man engaged in a game of chess.[5]

The Sultan's Retreat

One of the French Quarter's tallest and most imposing buildings has also held a dominating role in the area's legends and mysteries. Tradition maintains that the palatial edifice once witnessed a scene of rare carnage and hideous rape that still lingers within her massive, blood imbued walls.

These walls were constructed in 1836 by a wealthy and socially prominent Creole gentleman, one Jean Baptist Le Prete.[1] The mansion was of grand design. The polished hardwood floors reflected the delicate beauty of the imported lace and satin which adorned the sun filled, sparkling windows. Crystal chandeliers bathed the chateau with a galaxy of warm, inviting light. Jean Baptist's home was a center for the rich Creole culture which dominated the life of the French Quarter during the first half of the nineteenth century. If ever a home was built for cultured entertainment, such was the one created by the hand of Jean Baptist Le Prete.

Unfortunately for Monsieur Le Prete, the romantic culture of which he was so much a part started to wane during the second half of the century. Many Creole families began to lose the economic power they wielded for so long. As a result of changing fortune, many proud Creoles were forced to rent or sell their properties. Jean Baptist joined the ranks of his impoverished brethren, and was obliged to rent his home. Le Prete's tenant was a mysterious, grim Turk who claimed to be the deposed potentate of a distant eastern realm.[2]

The exotic Turk brought with him a fortune in gold and precious jewels. He established accounts at the largest banks and drew letters of unlimited credit. The "Sultan" began to use his great wealth to transform the Creole social palace into an Oriental pleasure palace. Heavy incense replaced light perfumes. A group of eunuchs catered to his needs. The gentile beauty of Creole finery was replaced by lavish Oriental accoutrements. The eunuchs were armed with wicked daggers and merciless swords. They patrolled the "Sultan's" property like soldiers. Where windows once opened to the clear sky, there were boarded and locked shutters. The iron gates surrounding the property were chained and locked. The enigmatic Turk had created a fortress, and lived within its walls like a general under siege. The new resident created a drum of security and silence about his person.

Of course, such activity aroused the interest and curiosity of his neighbors. Everyone was shocked by the change of character through which the palatial mansion had passed. A few scant weeks before the house was a center of light and festivity. Now, it stood dark and forbidding.

Within his web of privacy the Sultan had spun a world of mad delights. His retreat housed a substantial harem populated by women of all hues and sizes. Young Arab boys attended to the "Sultan's" less orthodox desires. Surrounded by opulence and guarded by fierce eunuchs, the dark Turk entertained passions too numerous and shocking to detail. His life seemed a blissful dream born through the narcotic vapors of a forbidden pipe.

One fateful night the reclusive pervert's utopia was ripped apart. As dawn ended that silent night, neighbors attending to their morning's business noticed rivulets of blood running from beneath the great, locked iron gates. The authorities were summoned. Upon their arrival they were met by barred doors. No amount of pounding could rouse the occupants. The police forced the doors. Inside the dark, incense laden rooms, the officers found a scene of utter catastrophe. A great battle had raged, consuming the lives of the "Sultan" and his entire retinue. Blood and viscera slickened the polished floors. Headless trunks and mangled limbs were scattered throughout the great house. No room was without a horror. The police soon realized that death had come to all the victims through sword or axe. No gunshots were fired which accounted for the relative silence of the butchery. It was impossible to say what body belonged with which head or limb. Even estimating the number that had been destroyed was complicated by the extent of the carnage. Body parts had been mutilated or burned to such a degree that an exact count of the dead could only be estimated.

The horror was not only confined to murder. The beautiful harem girls, the boys who entertained, and the eunuchs who protected the degenerate Sultan were subjected to vile sexual and physical assaults. The scandal was delicious. Stories of what happened on that dreadful night have fueled the imaginations and appetites of many an errant young man and wayward female to this very day.

The Turk's mutilated body was found buried in his garden. His suffering, contorted appearance testified that he had been buried alive. In his struggle to free himself from death's clutches he had partially torn himself from his premature grave. Unfortunately for the "Sultan," his efforts were too few, too late. He died suffocating on the rich, black, blood soaked soil of his garden.

The identity of the murderous fiends responsible for this hideous crime is open to historical conjecture. One theory holds that those responsible were members of some nefarious ship's crew. These devils had some dark business dealing with the reclusive, wealthy potentate. Upon realizing his enormous riches the ship's company devised a scheme of plunder, rape and homicide. They invaded his citadel and annihilated its protectors. With their safety assured, these blackguards tortured the "Sultan" and amused themselves with his concubinage. With the first rays of dawn they returned to their ship, the river and safety.[3]

Other opinions were certain that the marauders were assassins hired by the Turk's brother to avenge a theft and an insult. Seemingly, the "Sultan" had absconded with a fortune stolen from his sibling. The fortune's rightful owner searched the world for his felonious brother. Eventually, the thief was found ensconced in the Le Prete mansion. Having acquired this information, the brother sent his minions to New Orleans to reclaim the massive fortune and extract a brutal revenge.[4]

Whatever the facts are, they lie buried with the long dead players of this strange tale. What is a verifiable fact is that the LePrete house has a history of documented hauntings that extend through time to this very day.

The most recent cases involve two New Orleans residents, a Ms. Virgie Posten and a Mrs. Jean Damico. The first testimony comes from Ms. Posten who was a tenant in the old building during the late 1950's. In a Times Picayune interview[5] she went on record stating that during her tenure in a ground floor apartment she was startled numerous times by the appearance of a silent, lone male figure garbed in outlandish Oriental fashion. The figure disappeared as mysteriously as he appeared. These manifestations, unnerving as they were, did not force Ms. Posten from her apartment. Her haunted flat was close to her employment and inexpensive. These pragmatic concerns overshadowed whatever trepidation the restless shade engendered. She learned to coexist with the strange appearances until one fateful, fear filled night.

On the night in question Ms. Posten and a friend were spending a relaxed evening chatting about their careers and hopes for the future. The conversation was interrupted by the sound of footsteps in the hall outside of Virgie's door. The footsteps continued as if to indicate a nervous pacing back and forth. Investigation into the shadowy hall revealed no discernible presence. Ms. Posten theorized it was the mischievous ghost of her acquaintance up to his old tricks. She dismissed the incident and resumed her conversation. It was at this time that she and her friend were startled senseless by the most hideous, blood chilling scream she had ever heard. The power and

volume of the scream indicated more a beast from hell than a human source. The monstrous sound emanated from the bottom of a dark, spiral staircase, and waged itself through the entire building. In an instant faster than any rational reflection, Ms. Posten and her guest fled in total terror from the haunted abode never again to return.[6]

Approximately ten years later, another voice recounted an experience with the unknown terror that stalks the ancient palace. The voice belongs to Jean Damico. In 1966 she and her husband, Frank, and their business partner, Anthony Vesich, Jr., purchased the home in order to restore it and rent its many rooms. Mrs. Damico related that many of her new neighbors began to tell her about the building's bloody history, and the chain of peculiar events associated with her newly acquired property. At first, she dismissed the stories as just so much superstitious gossip that is sometimes associated with dilapi-dated old houses. That was until she, herself, began experienc-ing the appearances of our spectral visitor.

One night, while trying to sleep, Mrs. Damico became aware of a presence in her room. She opened her eyes and saw what appeared to be the figure of a man standing in the darkness at the foot of her bed. She lay perfectly still, gripped by sheer terror. After what seemed like an eternity the silent shape seemed to approach her. Summoning all of her courage she reached for her bedside lamp. Instantly, the room was flooded with light that revealed nothing out of the ordinary. The spectre had vanished.[7]

Mrs. Damico's story continues. She became aware of the history of her property. She learned about the "Sultan" and his mutilation and hasty burial. Through this knowledge she realized that a strange, twisted tree which grew in the courtyard emanated from the approximate site of the Turk's grave. Mrs. Damico remarked that the tree seems to be agonizing from the cursed soil to the outside street in much the same manner as the "Sultan" is reported to have done. Could it be that the spirit of his death agony has somehow become incarnate and manifest in the living tissue of this tree which takes its life from his al-most forgotten unhallowed grave?

The Sultan's Retreat is a story filled with intrigue, unan-swered questions and quite a store of documentation. In order to perhaps answer some questions and add to the anecdotal evidence the author attempted to interview Ms. Posten and Mrs. D'Amico. No trace could be found of Ms. Posten. The telephone book, directory assistance and all the usual avenues for finding individuals were exhausted.

Mrs. Damico was easy to find, or at least her name. She still resides in the old mansion; however, over a half a dozen visits and notes failed to elicit a response. I am sorry to conclude this story without an interview or investigation. Perhaps one day we will get a chance to roam the old rooms and corridors and maybe even meet the "Sultan" himself.

The Creole Lady

The following account chronicles the misadventures of a very malevolent and malignant spectre. It is also one of the city's least known and least documented ghost stories. In fact, the story is chronicled in only one source.[1] By itself, such scare documentation is unusual for a city that loves gossip almost as much as we love ghosts.

Our Royal Street Haunting traces its genesis to a suicide and a murder. The turn of the nineteenth century bore witness to the desperate, sadistic final act of a grand Creole lady whom legend recalls as Madame Mineurecanal. One troubled night, for reasons long forgot, the grand dame ascended the narrow staircase that leads to the third floor. In her unknown anguish she fastened a hemp rope to a secure overhead beam. Her lantern transformed the musty attic into a cave of shifting shades. The dark shadow of her trembling hands tested the rope, caressed the noose. She positioned a chair directly beneath the rope. She gazed at the noose.

Breath, the sound of breath tearing from a fear filled throat crawled through her ears. She paused. It was not her breath. Her eyes fell upon the cringing form of her faithful dog. The passion of her death fled from her heart to her hands. She felt the soft warmth of the little animal's throat. She felt his trachea crush and his spine snap. Silence.

Again, she turned to her desire for death. The rope scratched when she placed it around her noble neck. The body swayed as she pulled the noose tighter around her throat. In an instant, death began his embrace.

Madam M's death did not mark the end of her sinister existence. An entire family was witness to spectral experiences in the brooding, old manse. The documentation[2] begins with Ramon's testimony. Ramon, a New Orleans native of Creole extraction and former occupant of the Creole Lady's forlorn abode, related a strange tale. Throughout his childhood in the house he and his entire family were the subjects of an unrelenting reign of terror. Whenever he or his sister, Teresa, misbehaved they were punished by confinement on the second floor hallway. The hallway ended at the very stairway Madam M. climbed to meet her painful death.

As he and his sister sat in silence bathed by tears, they trembled. Their trembling stemmed not from the remorse they felt for some juvenile misdemeanor, but from the expectation of the terror filled apparition they knew they must soon witness. Their young eyes were riveted to the attic door. Within the youthful ears pulses of dark blood flowed in response to the frantic beating of their hearts. Suddenly, without warning, "she" appeared. A middle-aged woman with long wavy, dark hair descended from the black shadows of the staircase. Her eyes bulged from their sockets. Her swollen, clay-brown tongue protruded from her silent lips. A circle of torn, bloodied flesh marked her neck like some hideous necklace. Closer and closer she came to the petrified siblings. The smell of death preceded her. The fires of hell burned in her wild, black eyes. Slowly, her thin arms reached out, stretching, clutching at her young prey. No more! Screams, curses and a parental beating were better than this. Ramon and Teresa broke and ran. They ran down the stairs and out of the house accompanied by their screams of terror and despair.

The children were not the only residents of the house to be affected by the restless Creole lady. The children's mother, some seven months pregnant, was confronted by the spectre. Her encounter with the dreadful ghost almost stilled her heart. Two months later the child she was carrying was stillborn.

A young cousin spent some time with the afflicted family. The cousin, when told about the spectre of the grand old dame, made light of the story. He began a sing-song chant parodying her name - "Mini Canal, Mini Canal."

Shortly after the child retired for the night a scream echoed through the dark house. The family rushed to his room. They switched on the lights. The poor child was frozen with fear. A crimson imprint of a delicate hand marked the left side of his face. Evidently, Madame did not appreciate the child's juvenile disrespect.

The hauntings continued to the point where every family resident in the house of shame was affected. The children's father climbed into bed one night. He turned to embrace the figure lying next to him who he naturally assumed was his wife. His ardor turned to fear when he came face to face with a lifeless face from hell.

Several other family members reported an amazing array of classical ghost phenomena. Moans were heard in the dead of night. Cold spots, without explanation, chilled bodies and souls. The scampering feet of a dog could be heard scratching the attic floor. And finally, every family member swore to seeing the ghost of the dreadful woman at one time or another during their tenure in the house.

The house was investigated by Winer and Osborn.[3] These seasoned paranormal investigators became convinced that some unknown energy pervades the dwelling. After a period of investigation they told the present owner and the only "living" person in the house, except themselves, that they were leaving. They remarked that he did not have to disturb himself for they would let themselves out. As soon as they exited the front door, it slammed thunderously behind them. The authors left in amazement. Obviously, the Creole Lady dislikes intrusions.

The Sky Is Falling

History records thousands of instances of strange objects falling from the sky with no apparent cause. Fish, rocks, frogs, and all manner of unusual objects have descended from the heavens. The reality of these occurrences has been documented from ancient times to the present day.[1]

No doubt, fish and other aquatic creatures falling from the sky can be rationally explained. Atmospheric disturbances suck up large quantities of water and its inhabitants. This material may rise thousands of feet and travel over land for great distances. Then as the power of the disturbances wanes, the suspended material falls to earth where the superstitious either praise God or fear Satan.

Problems like this are easy to fit into our geometries of space and time. But, what about bricks or boulders falling from cloudless skies? New Orleans witnessed such an occurrence in 1890 in the 200 block of Cherokee Street located in the uptown Carrollton section of New Orleans. Old sources speak of the occurrence as a war between two ghosts. One of the spectral antagonists was a child by the name of Ollie Voss. The other was a grumpy old man, Abner White.[2] White was a hateful misanthrope who especially disliked children. He felt as though the children made fun of him and spread lies behind his back. One day as he was going about his business he was accidentally jostled by a group of giddy young girls. He turned his frustration and paranoia upon one child in particular - Ollie Voss. The child was literally throttled by the malevolent old maniac. His rasping voice brought the curse of God and Hell upon her soul. With contempt he flung her away from him and stormed away. Nothing was done about this attack because most in the neighborhood feared the old miser who carried a revolver and was dedicated to vengeance. Ollie avoided old Abner as did most of the other local youth. Unfortunately, Ollie's fear of Abner grew to abnormal dimensions. The old rascal seemed to sense this weakness and he exploited it. When by chance poor Ollie happened upon Abner, he would fix his baleful eyes upon her and send terror into her soul. The child lived a life of fear and panic in the shadow of Abner White whom she seemed to find in every part of her world.

Old Abner died. He died in his sleep leaving nothing to the world but a ramshackle house and many unpleasant memories. The neighborhood rejoiced. "This one-man reign of terror now must answer to God," the self-righteous declared.

Shortly after Abner's death, Ollie Voss was warming herself before retiring when a lava hot brick fell from the chimney sending burning charcoal and wood over the young girl's body. Her night clothes ignited like a torch. The poor child died shortly thereafter from her burns. The chilling part of this tale was that all the while the child burned to death she kept screaming, "It's old Abner White. He's there . . . it's old Abner White."[3]

Ollie was buried. The entire affair became a bitter, repressed memory. As time passed, the family tomb where Ollie lay decayed. Her remains, as well as those of her ancestors, were reinterred in a new tomb in a better maintained cemetery. Coincidentally, this new tomb was next to the sepulcher of old, hateful Abner White. It is from this point that our haunting takes form. Bricks and stones began to fall from the sky one dark night. In the morning the 200 block of Cherokee was a littered mess. The police investigated. The neighborhood was under surveillance. The next night was an exact reenactment.[4] Bricks, pieces of iron and slabs of mortar just seemed to fall from the sky. A falling stone even crushed the skull of a child, killing her within the hour.[5] For the better part of a week the missiles rained mercilessly.

Searching for explanations, those concerned believed that they were experiencing a ghost war. The sorrowful memory of Ollie and Abner's hatred was rekindled. It was revealed that on the day Ollie and her ancestors were coincidentally laid to rest next to the morose crypt of Abner White's, the hail of bricks and stones began. Acting upon these suppositions, Mr. and Mrs. Voss had their family remains once again moved. They sold the tomb. The barrages of debris ceased.[6]

The classical poltergeist occurrence has to do with apparently causeless flying objects, and the presence of a pre-pubescent or adolescent female. Perhaps ninety percent of this peculiar event is associated with a child who experiences a great deal of mental stress as her body begins to mature. However, it is always a living child, not one long dead. Also, the events seemed to be directed toward Ollie and her family rather than from them. It was her family's property that received the brunt of the attack. The yard and sidewalk where Ollie and her friends played jacks and had tea parties also suffered a greater than average bombardment. Logically (if such a word can be applied to such a situation) it would seem that Abner White was the antagonist. But, from what vantage point did he launch his war? And what fueled his war machine? These questions will probably remain unanswered for all time. All that can be added is, may Ollie and Abner rest in peace - where ever that peace may be.

The Family Ghost

Ghosts have dreadful reputations. They haunt houses and terrify the living with their caterwauling and mournful screams. Miscreant children are threatened with their vengeance. All in all, it seems ghosts should be avoided at any cost.

This feeling is not shared by Mrs. E., an uptown lady from an established family. She claims that the ghost who resides in her home, located somewhere in the uptown section of the city actually saved her father's life.[1] One afternoon in the 1950's, she and her mother went shopping, leaving her father at home alone. Mrs. E.'s father went to a back room to relax and watch television.

Soon, he drifted into a deep sleep. Suddenly, he was awakened by his name being called in an urgent voice. Still groggy, he glimpsed a female form standing in the hallway. Again, his name was urgently called. The female form disappeared down the hall. Being alarmed by these events, the gentleman rushed to the open door and peered down the hallway. He could just barely discern the woman at the hallway's end. His vision was hampered by a thick, gray cloud of acrid smoke. He hastily ran down the smoke-filled corridor to the front door. With gasps and burning eyes he fled to the street. The wail of sirens in the evening sunlight announced the arrival of the fire department. Upon recovery, Mrs. E.'s father began a frantic search through the crowd for his wife and family. Not finding them sent him into a panic. He rushed toward his flaming house only to be physically restrained by the firemen. In torment he screamed for his family. "Don't you understand - they're in there - my wife and child - they're in there," he pleaded.

Trying to calm the distraught man, the firemen vowed they would save his family. Unexpectedly, his wife and child exited the family car to witness a scene of chaos. Seeing his family safe, the man embraced them with joyous sobs of relief.

The woman responsible for saving the young father's life was the family ghost.[2] Mrs. E. does not know the identity of the ghost, but she believes the ghost is female and has been a part of her family for five generations. The ghost is in sympathy with the family. She foretells events such as deaths and births. Unfortunate occurrences are announced by unseen pacing and heavy footsteps on the hardwood floors and thuds to the doors and walls. This ghost is a benign spirit who actually gives great comfort to the family. Mrs. E. related several stories that have become part of her family's tradition. Older family members would soothe the various anxieties and fears of childhood by telling them that they had a very special guardian who would protect them during still hours of the night.

During a telephone interview, Mrs. E. gave me permission to visit her home and conduct my own investigations of what she said was a very active ghost. Sadly, Mrs. E. called me the next day to say that her family was totally against any investigations or interviews about such "nonsense" as ghosts. Mrs. E. is an educated, reputable businesswoman. Missing out on this interview was a great disappointment. Her testimony and the house itself would have presented some interesting data. Still, this story is important because of the reliability of the witness and the fact that it has been documented in the public record.[3]

The Gallows' Trap

Early in the morning while the mist still clings to the earth, a mind-shattering crash is sometimes heard ripping from the rear of an old antebellum building. The gallow's jaws slam open. A rope snaps taut. Human bones are splintered. It is the sound of death. The ghost that allegedly haunts the grounds of the stately old court house is no spectral image. This ghost takes another form. It is a ghost of sound. The echo from death that stalks the hours before dawn was born of a process - the process of lawful execution.[1] Some contemporary witnesses report the sound of heavy wooden doors being sprung. Others have given ghastly testimony, affirming the nauseating sound of a human being slowly chocking to death. Finally, some have experienced the melancholy melody of ancient Afro-American Gospel songs.

In 1833 Carrollton was created when one Charles Zimple laid out a township approximately five miles from the existing boundary of New Orleans. Two years later the New Orleans and Carrollton Railroad was constructed. That railroad still exists today as the St. Charles Avenue streetcar. It is the oldest continually running line of public transportation in North America. Zimple named his new town after General William Carroll, one of the heroes of the Battle of New Orleans. In January 1814 General Carroll was bivouacking there with a force of Tennessee militia and volunteers while awaiting further orders from General Andrew Jackson.

Zimple's little town grew rapidly.   By 1841 the town officially incorporated. Nine years later Carrollton had grown to such importance that it became the county seat of sprawling Jefferson Parish. In order to accommodate their new prestige and political power the citizens of Carrollton decided to create a town hall and administrative complex. Henry Howard was commissioned to design and construct the project in 1852. The result was a classic Greek Revival city hall and court house which stands to this day. Part of this administrative complex was a red brick, two-story jail. The jail, located on Hampson and Short Streets fronting on Hampson, remained in use until its demolition during the summer of 1937.

During its almost 85 year tenure, the jail was witness and participant to untold human misery. Within its sturdy walls perhaps as many as one thousand human beings met death. Suicides were commonplace. Disease and lack of medical attention contributed to their numbers. Violence claimed yet more lives. But the greatest fear inside those red brick walls was the gibbet. Virtually no week passed in those early years when the gallow's voice was silent. She was a lover of all humankind and rejected no one from the darkness of her womb. She

embraced coal black slaves and lily white gentlemen with the same passion. She even accommodated the rare female caller with no prejudice whatsoever. Literally hundreds fell through her lips into the void. Each was welcomed by the same sinister soul crushing crash. The best for which her long line of lovers could wish was a brief caress ending in an instantly broken neck and death. Sometimes her embrace would linger. The knot occasionally slipped from under the left jaw to the back of the head. In such a case the condemned was doomed to endure a strangulation that might consume as much as thirty minutes. On other dates the condemned prisoner's "drop" might be more than her neck could accommodate. The result of this miscalculation resulted in decapitation and one hell of a bloody mess. Whatever the outcome, the prisoner could rest assured that his dance with the gallows would be satisfying. He would never feel the urge to return.

Each crash announced the end of a fear-filled, wasted existence. Time and again wretched prisoners were led from one of the four death cells on the second floor into the early morning to face the noose. The prisoner, arms pinioned to his sides with leather straps, was led up the wooden steps. The

Negroes in their segregated cell block would sing gospel songs as the condemned was positioned on the double trap doors. His legs were strapped together at the knees and ankles. The death warrant was read. If any last words were to be uttered, now was the time. These formalities ended, a black mask was placed over the head. The noose was tightly adjusted to the rear of the left jaw. Suddenly, he who was about to die was alone. No hands bothered the quaking body. All around was blackness and silence. The only sound audible to the masked, bound figure was the sound of his own breath tearing from his dry throat into the moist blackness of the mask that hid his shameful head. Each second was an eternity. Where is the hangman? Is he pulling the lever? Maybe a last minute reprieve? What thoughts fired across that terror-filled brain is the privilege of those who have so died. We can only speculate in dread. Suddenly, the body started in fear as it plummeted into the black hole of the gallows' floor. As soon as the journey began it came to a jarring halt. The rope snapped taut. The suspended body began a series of convulsive jerks. Urine and feces filled the trousers of the dying wretch.

The attending physician would wait until the body ceased its shudders. He would then examine the suspended felon for a heart beat. If none were found, the body would be freed from the gallows' grasp and placed in a plain, pine coffin for a hasty burial. If, on the other hand, a heart beat was found, the body would be allowed to hang until that heroic organ was still. Such was a hanging.

If fear and terror can leave a trail anywhere, what better place than the path to execution? Many ghost stories are spun around a premature or violent death. Obviously, prisons, by their very nature, are likely candidates for spawning ghosts. The old Carrollton prison that was witness to so much human suffering was demolished decades ago. The complex of buildings that supported the mechanisms of government also fell victim to changing times. All that remains is the imposing antebellum court house and an echo that some say is the ghost sound of the dread gallows.[2]

Destrehan Manor

"**O**f course, every old plantation home in Louisiana has at least one ghost."[1] Stately, beautifully restored Destrehan Manor is no exception. This is a fresh story because the documentation is recent, and comes from those employed in this ancient tourist attraction.

The November 1, 1980 Times Picayune/States Item reported:

"They don't believe in Ghosts," but three women employees say a tall, thin man has been appearing and then disappearing mysteriously at the 193-year old Destrehan Manor.

'This isn't a hoax,' insisted Ann Little, administrator for the past five years at the elegant plantation at Destrehan about 15 miles up the Mississippi River from New Orleans.

Carol Schexnayder, assistant administrator, and Maxine Roberts, manager of the gift house, said they recently saw the apparition.

'I was walking from the gift shop to my office,' said Schexnayder. 'As I passed a window, I saw he wanted to come in, but when I opened the door to invite him in, he had disappeared.'

The two-story house has broad galleries and stately columns and is the centerpiece of an old plantation surrounded by a wrought iron fence - the sort of place where you'd expect to see a ghost, particularly around Halloween.

Schexnayder said she also saw the man about two hours later.

'Again, I was walking back from the gift shop,' she recalled. 'I saw the same man again, through the window at the front door. This time I ran and looked out the door. There wasn't anyone there. He was the same man wearing those black clothes.'"

'She came into the office trembling,' said Little.

Roberts said her experience was equally disturbing.

'I saw him later in the afternoon, at closing time,' she said. 'I peeked out of the window of the gift shop to see if the gates were locked, and they were. So I came to the office and I saw a man in dark clothes outside the window. When I got to the door, no one was there.'

'It gave me goose bumps,' said Roberts.

'What we must understand is that all of these things have been seen by people who don't really believe in ghosts,' said Little.

'Sure, we have a lot of reports of ghosts and eerie presences, but most of them come from people who come here with the idea that ghosts do really exist. I don't put a lot of faith in those kinds of sightings. But the people who work here don't generally believe in ghosts, so their sightings have us puzzled.'

Little said, however, that other experiences reported by workmen and tourists are often fascinating.

She recalled once that painters were working late and alone some years ago in an upstairs room and heard footsteps in an adjoining room. When they investigated, no one was there.

Years after that, Little recalled, a woman visitor interested in Jean Lafitte legends, looked up a fireplace and dared the legendary pirate to come out. A friend photographed the visitor and, when the film was developed, the ghostly face of a man looked out from a nearby mirror.

Then, she said, there was the movie crew that recently shot scenes at Destrehan Manor for a film about the life of voodoo queen, Marie Laveau. The crew left behind a black cat.

'The cat was acting rather strangely all day a couple of weeks ago,' said Little. 'She was prowling around the house, hissing at something. She wouldn't keep still.'

'Later that afternoon, I saw the darkly clothed man on the front porch. It was after closing time and the gates had already been locked, so I went to the door to investigate. When I opened the door, no one was there.'

'And the cat has never been seen since."

Antebellum plantations are fertile grounds for ghosts stories. They are all quite old and their histories are written in human blood and suffering. Virtually every plantation house boasts of a resident ghost or ghosts. In New Orleans the ghostly residents of Destrehan Manor are among the most famous and well known in the area. It should also be mentioned that Destrehan Plantation is an active tourist site and is quite accessible from New Orleans. For these various reasons the author elected to include the plantation in this effort.

On a glorious spring day in May 1990 the author, accompanied by his friend and photographer, Maury White-Hereford, traveled northwest along River Road to the old plantation. Upon our arrival we noted a sign that announced guided tours through the old home. The tour was informative, but no mention was made of any ghostly activity. Since my exclusive interest was ghosts I asked the guide about the haunting I had researched. She curtly told me she did not believe in such things, but if I was interested in such "foolishness" I could inquire at the gift shop.

The ladies in the gift shop were quite receptive to our questions - a welcome change in attitude from our somewhat abrupt guide. These cooperative employees told us that they, as well as a number of tourists, had actually experienced a variety of encounters that could only be described as supernatural. Cold spots, unexplained moans and groans, inexplicable lights and even photographic evidence were all part of the ghostly occurrences the gift shop employees shared with us. The photographic evidence was of particular interest to me. Prominently displayed on the shop's wall is a framed photograph of a young lady standing on the spiral staircase located at the plantation entrance. The young lady is a tourist. Directly behind and above her is a cloud with a distinct, disembodied head in its midst. At the time the photograph was taken, neither the young lady nor the photographer was aware of the anomaly. Upon developing the negative the tourist saw the "ghost." The picture was so clear and amazing that they sent a copy to the plantation. I inspected the photograph and took a picture of it. As can be seen through my second hand photograph the face is clear and very discernible. We took several pictures of our own in the same location in the hope of capturing the image directly. Haplessly, our efforts proved futile. Our cooperative employees said that the picture had been carefully analyzed by a laboratory. The analysis was unable to explain the phenomenon.

Beside the photographic evidence, the gift shop also sells a non-copyright story about the sightings for a mere seventy-five cents. I feel that it is appropriate to include this documentation because it helps to substantiate the validity of the haunting:

"It can happen any day at Destrehan Plantation Manor House. A visitor on a tour will quietly ask his/her tour guide 'Is this house haunted?' The tour guide will undoubtedly tell the visitor, 'Yes, there is a history of sightings here.'

Or, a visitor may tell his/her tour guide, 'I can sense when a ghost or spirit is near and there is one in this house.'

Then again, the office may receive a telephone call from a local resident that goes something like this: 'I was driving by the manor house last night and I saw something strange.'

It is not unusual and it has been happening for years.

The most active the ghostly apparition has been was during the major restoration of the manor house in 1984.

A former tour guide and the daughter of the caretaker who lived on the grounds seemed to be the focal point of all the activity. Annette Roper's first encounter with the ghostly figure was in May 1984 in her bedroom of the family trailer behind the manor house. It was 11 P.M. and she was in her bed reading. She turned over and saw a white, near transparent shape. She was terrified by the sight and it did not disappear until morning.

The next sighting by Annette was later in the month.

She was washing the car near dusk when she saw the white shape in the center second story window. This time he was wearing a hat. She watched as the figure, which was visible through several windows, descend the stairs. Annette ran to get one of her sisters, and together they saw it heading for the side gate. Then, around the end of June, she was watching for a friend to arrive at the same gate and again saw the shape cross the driveway.

Another member of the Robert family, Annette's cousin, was walking a dog on the grounds around Labor Day 1984 and came across the apparition. Annette's cousin has vowed never to return to the manor house.

It was also the Labor Day weekend in 1984 that a visitor had her picture taken on the newly restored staircase by a friend. When the picture was developed, what seemed to be a figure of a man was standing behind her. She sent the picture and the negative to the manor house office. It was investigated by experts to see if it was tampered with or if it was a reflection of light. All the experts said, "No!" The administration had the picture blown up and it is on display in the manor house gift shop.

Annette's final confrontation with the spirit was in March 1985. She was outside sitting on the tailgate of the family truck and she was alone. She heard a man's deep voice call out her name. The only man on the site was her father and he was inside. She ran inside and told her family, who said she cried all through dinner.

Although for years, the ghost at Destrehan Manor House was believed to be the privateer Jean Lafitte, it is believed that Annette's ghost is a former owner of the home, Stephen Henderson.

Henderson owned the plantation during in the early part of the 19th century and died in 1837. Annette is said to resemble Henderson's wife, Elenore Zelia Destrehan Henderson, who died in 1830 at the youthful age of 30. Bereaved by the death of his wife and restless after death because his controversial will was overturned, Henderson's spirit is believed to still walk the grounds of the manor house. Both Hendersons are buried in the near-by St. Charles Borromeo Catholic Church Cemetery.

Another vein of thought is that a figure dressed in a dark suit of clothes, which has been seen in the past, could be that of Lafitte, who was a frequent visitor to the house and a friend to Stephen Henderson.

More recently, a visitor on tour of the manor house saw a light apparition floating about the head of another young female tour guide. The tour guide later said that she felt nothing at the time the visitor saw the apparition. This took place in the restored stairway area.

One of the oldest and strangest ghost stories is that of a former owner, who eventually was taken to New Orleans where he spent his final years in a nursing home. Years after the man was taken to the nursing home, a reception was held at the manor house, which included a tour of the house. While the tour was being conducted by a servant, an unknown man, tall, thin and gaunt in appearance, joined the group. No one knew him. When asked who he was, he didn't reply. Just before the tour ended, he disappeared. Later, in telling of the incident, the servant described the man to his mistress. Upon checking, she was told that her husband had died at the nursing home at the precise time the unknown figure was seen walking among the reception guests.

A former employee of the manor house tells of several times when she saw a dark, shadowy figure of a tall, thin man through a window at the front door. When she would open the door, he would be gone.

There are several stories from visitors who hear footsteps and have mysterious quests on their tours. Another guest took a picture upstairs by a mantle with a mirror above it. When developed, the image of the face of a man appears in the mirror.

During the filming of a documentary about the life of voodoo queen, Marie Laveau, the crew left behind a black cat. Anne Little, a former administrator, claims that one day the cat was prowling around the house and hissing. Later in the same day, Anne saw the darkly clothed apparition on the front porch. Anne went to investigate and the man disappeared. The cat was never seen again.

The notoriety of the manor house and its ghost stories is spreading. It has been the subject of several newspaper articles and television news stories, especially around Halloween. Most recently, the manor house has been included in the book, *The Ghostly Register*, by Arthur Myers.

Most of the current staff and volunteers claim to have had at least one experience with the spirits at Destrehan. Some of them as simple as a cold pocket of air, a touch on the shoulder when they are all alone or an unidentifiable noise. The nursery and the restored interior stairway seem to be the places in the house most associated with the experiences.

As with all old homes, ghost stories are bound to develop. Although stories of spirits are fascinating, the manor house and its history are a marvel in itself. The majority of our visitors are interested primarily in the manor house and not its spirits. So, are there ghosts in Destrehan Plantation Manor House? You be the judge!"[2]

The sheer volume of witnesses, the photographic evidence and the large amount of documentation all contribute to a very convincing case for the actual existence of ghostly visitors. Although this author did not witness any paranormal manifestation, it is his firm belief that Destrehan Plantation holds many secrets yet to be divulged.

The Ghost In The Photo

S ince 1979, during Halloween weekends, I have been a guest on Joe Culotta's popular New Orleans radio talk show, "Let's Talk It Over."[1] After my guest spot, Halloween 1990, I was approached by a gentleman who was to be a guest on the show later that day. He introduced himself as Remy A. Bosio. Mr. Bosio is a medical technician at the Veteran's Hospital in New Orleans. He related a story that was told to him by his friend, a Mr. Fritz Broom. Mr. Bosio also presented me with a photograph that allegedly reveals the ghostly form of a young girl in period costume. The photo was taken by Mr. Bosio's friend, Fritz Broom.

Mr. Broom agreed to create a narrative to explain how he came to take the picture and why he is convinced it holds the image of a ghost. The following is the full and complete text of the account he submitted to me:

In the summer of 1989 my family, Vicky my wife, Jennifer my daughter, Jason my son and myself, Fritz Broom, had planned a vacation in Houston, Texas with our friends Jack and Linda Taylor and their daughter Jackie. We were to spend a couple of days at Astro-World and Water World. But because of a hurricane that suddenly moved from out of the Gulf of Mexico to directly over Houston, we wound up spending only one night there. Because of the severe weather conditions we decided to head back home and on the way visit my brother-in-law, Joe, in Lafayette.

While at Joe's house we decided to visit some of the Plantations in St. Francisville on our way back to Chalmette. It was something we had always wanted to do and everyone agreed.

We visited Greenwood Plantation first which was used in the mini-series "North and South." This is a Greek Revival style plantation with large columns all around. This is the type of plantation that most people picture in their minds when they think of a plantation. After leaving Greenwood we headed for the Myrtles Plantation.

Before arriving at the Myrtles we didn't know much about it or how it looked. We thought all plantations had the large columns and porch all around. We hadn't heard any ghost stories about it except that it's a bed and breakfast place with reenactments of some murder mysteries that had happened in the house.

When we turned off the highway onto the driveway leading to the Myrtles we all commented on how eerie and dark it looked. We guessed that is why it has the nickname "The Dark Lady." I parked the van at the side of the house and we walked under the oaks leading to the front of the house. My daughter Jennifer took a couple of pictures of the front of the house, one as my son Jason, and Linda and Jackie Taylor were going up the front steps. We also took several other pictures inside the home. Jason Broom and Jackie Taylor were the first on the front porch and pressed the door bell.

The tour guide opened the door about one minute later and invited us in. After we were all in the central hall we could see into most of the large rooms in the front of the house and we were the only visitors there at that time.

The tour guide started her tour with the statement that she would not tell any ghost stories, because the owner did not want visitors coming to the Myrtles for ghosts, but for its historical value. She had really gotten our curiosity up. We all began asking about the house and its history. She finally gave in and quietly told us some of the stories. The original owner built the first part of the house in the 1700's and the rest was

added on by subsequent owners. She also told us that the
Smithsonian Institution spent several days in the house researching the hauntings of the house and declared it the most
haunted house in the United States. The guide said she had
heard several things in the house: voices, piano playing and a
baby crying. Once when in the house alone she heard
someone calling her name yet she knew for sure she was alone.
She immediately ran from the house to a neighboring house
and called someone to stay with her.

Another story she told us was about one of the plantation owners during slavery times who had a black mistress who was allowed to work in the house. He caught her eavesdropping on a conversation he was having with some gentlemen and as a punishment for this he cut one of her ears off and put her out of the house into the kitchen. Later she baked a cake with Oleander leaves as an ingredient. Pretending to make up with him she put it on the dinner table. But the master had left the plantation that day and after dinner his wife and two daughters ate some of the cake and died. One of the girls was named Sara.

At another time a young girl named "Sara" was very sick with yellow fever and the doctor had given up. The father of the girl, not wanting to give up on her, sent for a Voodoo woman to save her. The Voodoo woman said she could save her and stayed at the girl's bedside all night working her magic, but Sara died. Her father, being out of his mind, hung the Voodoo woman there in Sara's room. The Voodoo woman is one of the ghosts people claim to have seen in a bedroom upstairs.

We believe that the figure in our picture is one of the girls named Sara, and we call her "Sara." The four of our group who saw her: Jason, Jackie, Linda and Jack, said she waved to them as they climbed the front steps. Discussing what there had seen they agreed she had on an old-style dress with large puffy sleeves. We all agree this is an incident we will never forget.

In conclusion I might add Mr. Bosio is also an amateur scientist who is involved with astronomy, photography and a number of other scientific pursuits. He subjected the negative to various analytical procedures. At the end of his tests he reached the conclusion that the figure represented a human being of three dimensions and not simply a reflection or some light anomaly. Mr. Bosio is a technician who has the utmost respect for the scientific method. I have spoken with him at length both personally and via telephone. Each interview impressed me with his sincerity, knowledge and honesty. I believe the photograph is authentic. My belief is so secure that I have included it in this work and will gladly allow any competent individual or laboratory to examine it.

The Legacy of Marie Laveau

No book about the ghosts and haunted environs of New Orleans could possibly be considered complete without mention of the city's infamous witch queen, Marie Laveau. The story of Marie's life is as fascinating and strange as the ghost story which keeps her name and legend frighteningly alive in this "City that care forgot."

The woman destined to become New Orleans' most well-known occult personality was generated from jumbled beginnings. She was a free woman of color who was born either in New Orleans or Santo Domingo sometime around 1794.[1] Her father was probably Caucasian. Who he was is lost in the abyss of time. From all accounts, and from the faded portrait hanging in the Cabildo Museum in New Orleans, she was an attractive, fair complexioned mulatto. Her vocation was that of a hairdresser, a trade she much used to her monetary betterment as we shall see later on. It is recorded that she married on 4 August 1819, to one Jacques Paris, a free Afro-American. Her marriage was officiated by Pere Antoine, and was fully sanctioned by the Roman Catholic Church. In 1826 her marriage was dissolved by death. In that same year she began a lifelong relationship with Christope Glapion, also a free black. There are no records to indicate that this relationship was legitimized by the offices of the Church. February 1827 marked the birth of her daughter, namesake and heir to her occult empire. It is unknown if Marie Jr.'s father was Paris or Glapion. Marie's pregnancy overlapped Paris's death and her relationship with Glapion.[2] During her long life (1794-1881) she gave birth to fifteen children.

It is curious to note that her interest in Voodoo dates from the year 1826, the year her legal husband died. Perhaps her interest in the secrets of Voodoo were an attempt to fathom the mysteries of death which so unfortunately claimed her late husband? Or, maybe, this predilection was part of her possible West Indian background? What ever the reason for her interest in this dark religion was known only to Marie, and that knowledge lies silent in her grave. Voodoo, like Christianity, is syncretic. That is, it is composed of many elements appropriated from other faiths. The original animism of West Africa imported with the wretched slaves mingled with Roman Catholicism and Native American Indian practices to form a unique and bizarre theology. Voodoo is primarily matriarchal, and concerned with fertility and abandoned sexuality. Its history in the New World reaches back almost four hundred years. The practice brought faith and comfort, as well as fear and terror, to the countless slaves and numerous whites who fell under its influence. While it was most common among Afro-Americans, it also found a substantial number of whites who abandoned themselves to the dark embrace of this sensual theology. An old account published in the Times of 21 March 1869, bears witness to this reality:

"These women were all dressed elaborately, some of them in bridal costumes, and with an extraordinary regard for the fineness and purity of their linen. At one end of the chapel a corpse was exposed. The rites having been commenced, an elderly turbaned female dressed in yellow and red (Marie Laveau), ascended a sort of dais and chanted a wild sort of fetish song, to which the others kept up an accompaniment with their voices and with a drum-like beat of their hands and feet. At the same time, they commenced to move in a circle while gradu-

ally increasing the time. As the motion gained in intensity the flowers and other ornaments disappeared from their hair, and their dresses were torn open, and each one conducted herself like a bacchante. Everyone was becoming drunk and intoxicated with the prevailing madness and excitement. As they danced in a circle, in the center of which was a basket with a dozen hissing snakes whose heads were projecting from the cover, each corybante touched a serpent's head with her brand. In the midst of the Saturnalia of witches, the pythoness of this extraordinary dance and revel was a young girl, with bare feet, and costumed 'en chemise.'

In one hand she held a torch, and with wild, maniacal gestures headed the band. In this awful state of nudity she continued her ever-increasing frantic movements until reason itself abandoned its earthly tenement. In a convulsive fit she finally fell, foaming at the mouth like one possessed, and it was only then that the mad carnival found a pause. The girl was torn half-dead from the scene, and she has never yet been restored to her faculties."[3]

Another source testifies to the biracial character of these revelries. No doubt, a very shocking situation to nineteenth century decorum and racism.

"In 1855, when Captain Eugene Mazaret of the Third District police invaded a house of the Voodoo doctor Don Pedro, he found a dozen white women and as many Negro men, the former naked except for thin camisoles, and all busily amusing themselves and one another under the direction of the magician. They were all arrested and fined, although Doctor Don Pedro protested that they were simply undergoing treatment for rheumatism.

Next day the husband of one of the women committed suicide."[4]

Marie was the undisputed queen of a dark, forbidden counter culture. As a hair dresser of talent she had access to the most fashionable homes. She also employed her numerous daughters and followers as hairdressers, who conspired to form an intelligence network that bestowed legendary psychic powers to their employer. Marie's entrepreneurial enterprise did not end there. Her reputation as a madame and procurer

was well founded. Many an octoroon or quadroon beauty found a Creole dandy as her paramour through Marie's generous efforts.

Marie Laveau was a free woman of color who flourished and became a legend and power in a racist, segregated society. I believe this fact alone substantiates the vitality and strength of her will. She must have been an absolutely astounding woman.

Marie was more than just a practitioner of Voodoo. Her imaginative mind contributed to the theology of her faith. It was Marie who instituted the Virgin Mary as a central figure in Voodoo worship as well as the veneration of several Catholic saints. She borrowed freely from Catholicism as Catholicism had done with the Greco-Roman and Celtic religions it eventually superseded. She was instrumental in the formalization of certain dogmas and rituals that had heretofore been fragmented and disorganized. Had she been literately inclined she may have been to Voodoo what Saint Paul was to Christianity. Nevertheless, her influence lives on in the religion she helped to create and formalize.

Marie departed this life 15 June 1881. Her daughter, namesake and successor followed her several decades later. It is from the silent, secret dark abyss of death that Marie and her daughter allegedly still reign as ghost queens over spirit orgies in the ancient Saint Louis Cemetery #1. Both Maries are entombed in this cemetery which is the oldest existing kirkyard in the city. Each reposes in a separate, two-tiered, well maintained, white masonry structure. At first glance, they are indistinguishable from their neighbors. Upon closer examination one is struck by the fact that these graves are virtually covered with chalk and red brick markings.

Staggered rows of crudely etched crucifixes predominate. Most are traditional, but a few are inverted. Some display a Greek influence. Others bespeak a Celtic accent. Still others take the form of the Balken Kruse of German lore. The predominating pattern of the eldrich graffiti is a row of three traditional, upright crosses. Possibly, these patterns of three reflect a belief in the Christian concept of the Trinity. In Magical/Voodoo belief the number three signifies creation.[5] Whatever their meaning, the crosses present a strange anachronism in a world dominated by technology and skyscrapers.

Apart from the crosses, the tombs also display a variety of bizarre artifacts. Coins of various denominations arranged in geometric patterns can be seen along the marble borders. Pieces of herbs twisted in colored flannel send their subtle aromas into the hot, heavy southern air. Bricks wrapped in aluminum foil stand guard outside the sepulchers. Beans, bones, bags and all manner of bric-a-brac can be found

swearing mute testimony to the practice of ancient and arcane rituals which are still commonplace in this decaying city of the dead.

One basic reason for all of this occult supplication is the fact that many believe Marie returns to life to once again lead her faithful on St. John's Eve. During her return the tribute left by her faithful is thought to be sanctified. Through this act the living are believed to obtain communion with Marie and the world beyond death.

One young man, a vagrant during the 1930's, reported a tale of dread and terror. Being unemployed and living in the depths of the Great Depression the hapless witness decided to spend the night in the old cemetery. He scaled a tomb. For several hours he slept fitfully. Electrically, he was awoken. His brain thundered with the sounds of primitive drums and ecstatic chants. Fearing robbers, or perhaps a band of maniacs, he stealthily descended his sanctuary. Carefully he crept among the dark tombs hoping to find an exit and the relative safety of the streets. He turned a corner and was instantly bathed in a spectacle from the bowels of hell. Surrounding the cross splattered witch queen's tomb were ectoplasmic bodies of naked men and women engaging in passionate embraces and lustful postures. Rising from the midsts of this bacchanal stood a statuesque, nude, sepia woman entwined by a gigantic serpent. Her presence dominated the scene. It was from her being that this spectacle of sexuality and depravity seemed to rise. Before his terror laden eyes, freed from the fetters of death, stood Marie in all her splendor leading her ever faithful in a celebration of sensuality, concupiscence and fertility. The scene overwhelmed him. He fled for his life, his sanity, his soul.[6]

Another account states that three young men tasted tragedy because of Marie's sepulcher. The gentlemen in question had spent a constructive evening in the French Quarter - drinking and carousing. Becoming drunk and bored, their talk turned to death and witches and Marie Laveau. Before too long one of the trio was enticed into a wager. Thirty dollars said he would not have the courage to climb the cemetery's wall and drive an iron spike in old Marie's final resting place. With thirty dollars as a reward the young man threw himself over the wall.

His friends waited for his return. The minutes stretched to an hour. The inebriated fools called to their friend. No answer. They waited. They drank. They cursed. Dawn came, and with it, the opening of the cemetery's gates. The angry young men rushed to the grave waiting to vent their rage on their inconsiderate comrade. They found him by the side of the witch's grave - dead!

In his drunken state he hammered the spike through his coat and into the stone sarcophagus. As he rose to leave and collect his thirty dollars, some unseen force held him in place -- obviously his misdirected nail. Panic and fear must have raped his drunken, confused mind. He panicked. His struggle was in vain. Who knows what his mind conjured before him in the city of death? What ever it was, the power of his illusions were so strong that his alcohol stressed heart exploded. When discovered, his friends were aghast at the horror that was etched upon his wretched face.[7]

Whatever the truth really is concerning the hauntings of St. Louis Cemetery #1 and the witch queen who allegedly orchestrates them, one fact is certain and verifiable. The cemetery is a hotbed of a continuing tradition of Voodoo that reaches back almost four centuries. The faithful still flock to Marie's grave to offer dark sacrifices and occult supplications. Perhaps in this maelstrom of superstition Marie actually does rise from her grave on Saint John's Eve to preside over an orgy of the dead. Perhaps. . .well, who can really say?

Be it Remembered, That on this day, to wit this Sixteenth day of June in the year of our Lord One Thousand Eight Hundred and Eighty one, and the One Hundred and _____ of the Independence of the United States of America, before me, JOSEPH JONES, M. D., President Board of Health and Ex-Officio Recorder of Births, Deaths and Marriages, in and for the Parish of Orleans, personally appeared:

_____ Lamothe _____, a native of _____

residing at No. 152 St. Ann Street who hereby declares, that

Marie Glapion born Laveau (Creole)

a native of _____ _____ aged 98 years,

departed this life, yesterday (15th June 1881) at his afore-said residence in this city

Cause of Death _____

Certificate of Dr. John Coll. M.D.

This done at New Orleans, in the presence of the aforesaid _____ Lamothe, also in that of Messrs. Ph. Boublet & C. M. Lamana lath of this City witnesses by me required so to be, who have hereunto set these hands, together with me, after reading hereof, the day, month and year first above written.

_____ Lamothe
Ph. Boublet
C. M. Lamana
Joseph Jones M.D.

Epilogue

New Orleans Ghosts relates and documents twenty of the city's better known ghost stories. It is by no means complete. While investigating the material contained in this work the author was informed by various sources of over two dozen other, lesser well-known spook sites. Space and time have limited our effort to what is contained in these pages.

It is our sincere hope that New Orleans Ghosts was entertaining and perhaps even thought provoking. Ghosts and hauntings have been associated with every known culture. It is also an established fact that a large percentage of the human race finds a certain fascination in the uncertain, enigmatic realm of phantoms, ghosts and spectres. We know through anthropological research that Paleolithic humans offered sacrifices and created talismans and rituals to appease or control the spirits of the dead. We also know that the sundry religions of modern cultures devote a substantial amount of time and activity in order to insure that the dead will "rest in peace." It is absolutely amazing that the human race should have carried such supernatural baggage for tens of thousands of years without that baggage having some value or validity.

Using this perspective one must ultimately be forced to ask the question, "Are ghosts real?"

As with any question, we must apply a methodology in order to begin to frame an answer. It is this author's conviction that the only viable methodology available to extract truth from hair-brained conjecture or groundless faith is the utilization of the scientific method. Granted, the scientific method is not perfect, but it is the only methodology the human race possesses that can illumine truth through demonstrable consistent results.

The scientific investigation of paranormal activity is fairly recent. The first organized, scientific effort was the Society for Psychical Research founded by Sir William Crookes in 1882.[1] From those early days science has made great strides in answering many occult questions. Essentially speaking, paranormal or Psi researchers have evolved a set of theories which attempt to categorize and explain paranormal activities. For lack of any better or more descriptive terms we will call these two sets of theories the rational set and the occult or hidden set.

The rational set of theories claims that all paranormal activity can be explained in terms of existing laws and knowledge in a reasoned and rational way. One element of the rational set of theories declares that alleged spectral occurrences are nothing more than misinterpreted physical phenomena, for instance, ball lightening, bioluminescence or methane (swamp) gas. Our first story, "The Flaming Tomb," offers a partial validation for this concept. As you remember, Mr. Gandolfo, longtime cemetery employee, explained the red flashing light apparently coming from the tomb as the result of a red, flashing signal light. When the light was removed the phenomenon ceased. Atmospheric disturbances, as well as misinterpreted sense of impressions, have, no doubt, created many ghosts and ghouls, not to mention gods and goddesses.

Another component of the rational theory dictates that paranormal scenarios are the result of some neural pathology on the part of the observer. It is an accepted fact that drugs, trauma, stress, etc., can cause strange aberrations in our consciousness. It then stands to reason that an individual so impaired cannot be expected to give unprejudiced testimony. For example, our last story about the alleged activities of Marie Laveau were sustained by two sets of questionable witnesses. One witness was a vagrant who more than likely suffered the stress and undernourishment which is the hapless plight of the homeless through the ages. The other witnesses and "victim" were all intoxicated. Enough said.

Following the lines of logic, reason and established scientific laws and axioms there is also another important theory about the denizens of the land of the dead that is very rarely voiced. For many of us, ghosts exist out of fear and hope.[2]

There exists within all of us a certain "dark side" which enjoys fear. All we have to do is examine our own culture to see the strength of the shadows. We all enjoy being frightened, at least somewhat, whether we care to admit it or not. We keep ghost stories "alive" because we like scary things. A perfect illustration for this theory is "El Viejo Garrison de España." Here is a ghost story predicated on atrocious events which never transpired. Yet while researching this story several individuals swore that their parents or grandparents witnessed the bloody mutiny with its ghostly players on numerous occasions. Each "second hand" witness took great delight in relating this perverse tale of mutilation and torture.

Hope, in this instance, can be defined as a philosophical, existential predicate. Ghosts, or at least the belief in them, can be considered a death denial system. If ghosts exist, and if they are a reverent of human life, then we can rest assured that at least some species of life exist after death. One can gain great comfort in knowing that one's loved ones and eventually he or she will continue as a recognizable aspect of that former life that was so well known and loved. This affective response contributes its share to populating our world with ghosts and perhaps more importantly with keeping ghosts alive.

I think the "Octoroon Mistress" falls into this category. Everyone can relate to the "real" passion of love and especially frustrated love. For many of us, being in love and being loved is that situation which validates our lives. It is the thing that reminds us of life and the joy of being alive. So its not too far fetched for us to create a kind of wishful immortality when we see love consumed by death. Someone dies because of love, but that life affirming love is so real and so valid that it actually transcends the bonds of death. Presto - through our hope we have given birth to a ghost.

The rational theories deny any cause except one that fits into our present set of established scientific facts. It is the opinion of this author that these theories explain a very large portion of spectral phenomena. The point in fact is that most ghost stories do have a logical, reasonable explanation.

The second set of theories we refer to as the occult or hidden theories. In order to understand the nature of these theories it is first necessary to reflect a little further on the basis of the rational theories. Let us remember that the rational explanations are simply explanations that fit into our accepted concepts about the scientific method and the cause and effect scenario. True, most ghost sightings can readily be explained in terms of rational or established cause and effect relationships. The question now arises, what about those experiences which are outside scientific expectations? The true skeptic will maintain that such an occurrence is impossible. He will say we are simply victims of incomplete or prejudicial data. The place of the skeptic is somewhat sacred ground for without skepticism humankind would still be chanting Latin masses and languishing in a dark age. As with all areas of life and endeavor, we must be critical with our thoughts and acceptance. We must also be critical of our skepticism. Absolute skepticism would freeze all further human progress into the narrow confines of accepted axioms and laws and allow for no variation except for that which is written. Skepticism, then, must be tempered with a critical flame. When all possible "rational" explanations of a particular event have been exhausted it is time to begin creating new paradigms which upon their validation increase the sphere of the so-called rational.

One theory which has yet to be proved rationally holds that hauntings and poltergeist occurrences are actually manifestations of mental powers yet discovered. Hypnosis was known and practiced by priests and magicians for thousands of years before it was investigated by modern science and incorporated into the methods of medical practice. Hypnosis is still a mystery, but its existence and efficacy are established scientific facts.

Let us examine this idea from a slightly different perspective. Colin Wilson, in his most ambitious work yet, *Mysteries*,[3] quotes the occult work of Thomas Lethbridge.[4] Lethbridge had established himself as a professional archaeologist at the prestigious University at Cambridge, England before he became interested in paranormal phenomena in the early 1950's. His work began with experiments in dowsing and pendulum activity. From this work he eventually developed a theory concerning electromagnetism which could conceivably be a partial explanation for spectral manifestations. Basically Lethbridge proposes that the electromagnetic fields which encompass all matter have the property of absorbing influences from other electromagnetic fields. More specifically, he theorizes that the electromagnetic fields of humans, and in some instances animals, can under certain conditions of great stress or trauma coupled with conducive secondary atmospheric conditions, produce a species of recording on their immediate environment. It is worthwhile noting that Lethbridge feels that these fields are especially malleable where water is present, For instance, England, a wet, damp, water imbibed land, has more ghosts per acre than any other locality. New Orleans, by the same token, has more than its share of ghosts and goblins.[5] When we consider what we "know" about ghosts, a tape recorder or holograph representation seems a likely analogy. Many ghosts seem to reenact the same drama time and again in the same locality. Ghosts are usually determined and very predictable. On certain occasions, for instance the anniversary of the tragedy, a ghost will make its appearance, dance through its routine and fade into the woodwork. This has all the earmarks of an eight o'clock movie.

The exact mechanism for this species of event is unknown, but that's all right. No one knows how electricity really works, but we use and control it. Perhaps with the suitable technology we could learn to manipulate these peculiar events and open horizons as fascinating as electronics is today. Electromagnetic radiation may be the vibrations which excite our yet to be proved sixth sense which some theorists believe reside in the pineal gland. Such a theory might comfortably fit into a slightly expanded scientific view of electromagnetic theory.

Poorly understood powers of the mind such as hypnosis and Thomas Lethbridge's theories could offer plausible explanations for "The Family Ghost," and "The Sultan's Retreat." Respectively, "The Family Ghost" limits her activities to the members of one, specific family exclusively. This "ghost" could be guidance not of an entity from the realm of the dead, but of a yet uncharted species of psychic communication among living human beings. The spectral form witnessed by various family members might possibly be an empty vehicle somehow projected from the mind of one family member to others for the purpose of "objectivizing" a psychic message. Bizarre as this sounds, we must remember that scientists inform us that we use less than ten percent of our brain's mass. What potentials and secrets lay hidden in the other ninety percent of that remarkable organ?

Our research into the haunting entitled, "The Sultan's Retreat" is filled with evidence that seems to come verbatim from Professor Lethbridge's ideas. The alleged "Sultan" suffered a traumatic, vile death. The scene of the murder was charged with the basest of human emotions and passions. Where the carnage and murders were committed is but a few scant blocks from the Mississippi River, and is one of the dampest and most humid areas of the city. Finally, the apparitions and their attendant cacophony are not directed at any particular individual. The phenomena is non-intensive. Maybe Professor Lethbridge has discovered some strange truth about certain occult properties exhibited by certain sections of our environment.

Another theory which also deals with some yet undiscovered type of electromagnetic energy has to do with the poltergeist phenomenon. There exists a wealth of documented cases describing this activity.[6] In almost all of its manifestations, poltergeist phenomena seem to be related to an adolescent, usually female, who is undergoing a great deal of stress. Through some uncharted tributary the energy produced through stress and glands finds its expression in objective reality with somewhat startling results. Again the cause is unknown, but the effect has been well documented and scientifically studied. Unfortunately, the results of poltergeist studies are far from conclusive or even completely convincing. Evidently more research with refined methods and materials is needed before any conclusion can in part explain or possibly predict and/or control these peculiar documented effects. Poor, little Ollie Voss was an adolescent female. Through her unfortunate encounters with her nemesis, Abner White, she suffered an undue amount of anxiety and stress. What follows is a classical poltergeist tale with one remarkable exception. When the stones, bricks and debris began to batter the Voss residence, both Abner White and Ollie Voss were dead and buried. Here we are faced with a strange tale about an equally strange event.

The last theory states that apparitions are actually entities from another world, or more correctly, another dimension. In a sense, this is a back-to-square-one theory. Our Paleolithic ancestors believed that the spooks and demons, nymphs and salamanders that they tried to placate were actual "living" beings from another world. At certain times these beings could enter our world and interact with its inhabitants.[7] If these entities exist perhaps they might be the "souls" of the dead or some type of mysterious, non-physical intelligence. Perhaps . . . well, who can really say? The universe has yet to reveal to us even a microfraction of its vast secrets.[8] Possibly Shakespeare said it best, "There are stranger things in heaven and earth . . ."

As aforementioned, this author espouses the belief that the vast majority of spectral occurrences can be explained within the framework of our existing scientific laws and axioms. However, there is a certain percentage of these phenomena which cannot be so simply dismissed. What about cases where animals are terrified by certain rooms or locations, q.v. Consider also photographs which display peculiar shapes or shadows which, despite highly scientific and technical analysis, still retain their secrets, q.v. The exceptions to the rule, so to speak, could go on and on for virtually volumes. This is not our purpose. Essentially, all we have attempted to show is that there are several possible theories to explain otherwise inexplicable data. Their veracity can only be tested through time and objective reflection. It is enough here that we raise questions and stimulate interest. Through such efforts, one day may come realizations about our universe and our place in that universe that will forever transform the experience which we call human.

Acknowledgements

Tulane University, Louisiana Collection
Judy Finlandia, Typist
The people of New Orleans—past and present

Footnotes

I. Introduction

1. Jeanne de Lavigne, *Ghost Stories of Old New Orleans* (New York, New York: Rinehart & Company, Inc., 1946), p. ix.
   Richard Winer and Nancy Osborn, *Haunted Houses* (New York, New York: Bantam Books, Inc., 1980), p. 93.
   Lyle Saxon, *Gumbo Ya-Ya* (Canbridge, Massachusetts: The Riverside Press, 1945), p. 279.
2. de Lavigne, op. cit.
3. Joseph Campbell with Bill Moyers, *The Power of Myth* (New York, New York: Doubleday, 1988), pp. 5-8.

II. The Flaming Tomb

1. Mel Leavitt, *Great Characters of New Orleans* (San Francisco Lexikos, 1984), pp. 28-29.
2. Henri A. Gandolfo, *Metairie Cemetery: An Historical Memoir* (New Orleans: Steward Enterprises, Inc., 1981), p. 65.
3. Gandolfo, op. cit., p. 65.
4. deLavigne, op. cit., pp. 192-193.
5. de Lavigne, ibid., pp. 194-197.
6. Gandolfo, op. cit., pp. 65-66.
7. Gandolfo, op. cit.

III. LaMaison Lalaurie

1. de Lavigne, op. cit., p. 248.
2. de Lavigne, ibid., p. 250.
3. de Lavigne, ibid., p. 257.
4. de Lavigne, ibid., p. 258.
   Saxon, op. cit., p. 293.
5. Leonard V., Hubert, *New Orleans: A Pictorial History* (New York, New York: Crown Publishers, Inc., 1971), p. 127.

IV. A Haunted House

1. Information gathered through a personal interview with Mr. J.
2. Many reports of ghostly activity indicate that the ghosts encountered are non-interactive and extremely deterministic.
3. The class was an adult education class taught by Mr. Joe Culotta.
4. Among other graduate degrees, this author holds an M.Ed. in counselor education conferred by Loyola University of the South. He also is a Louisiana State certified counselor who has approximately ten years of psychological counseling experience.

V. The Reverend's Restless Wife

1. Opinion voiced by Ms. Sandra Roberts.

VI. The Ghostly Mariner

1. Mary Foster, "Spook Houses," *The Times-Picayune*, 31 October 1987.

VII. The Undead Comrades

1. Winer and Osborne, op. cit., p. 98.
2. de Lavigne, op. cit., p. 38.
3. Ibid., p. 38.
4. Winer and Osborn, op. cit., p. 99.
5. de Lavigne, op. cit., p. 37.
6. Ibid., p. 37.
   Winer and Osborn, op. cit., pp. 99-100.
7. Margaret Fuller, "Drops of Blood," *The Times-Picayune*, 10 November 1979.

VIII. The Deadly Dentist

1.   Saxon, op. cit. p. 295.
2.   Suzanne Stouse, "Tales to Tell on Halloween," *The Times-Picayune,* 25 October 1989.
3.   Saxon, op. cit., p. 294.
4.   Ibid., p. 294.

IX. Penelope

1.   Tricon House, a short pamphlet published by Tricon House, 711 Bourbon Street, New Orleans.

X. El Viejo Garrison de Espana

1.   Joan B. Garvey and Mary Lou Widmar, *Beautiful Crescent: A History of New Orleans* (New Orleans: Gramer Press, Inc., 1984), p. 42.
2.   de Lavigne, op. cit., pp. 281-284.
     Saxon, op. cit., pp. 295-296.
3.   de Lavigne, op. cit., pp. 281-282.
4.   Ibid., pp. 282-283.
5.   Saxon, op. cit., p. 296.
6.   de Lavigne, op. cit., pp. 281-284.

XI. Pere Dagobert

1.   de Lavigne, op. cit., p. 3.
2.   Walter G. Cowen, et al., *New Orleans Yesterday and Today* (Baton Rouge, La. and London: Louisiana State University Press, 1983), p. 12.
3.   Joan B. Garvey and Mary Lou Widmer, *Beautiful Crescent: A History of New Orleans* (New Orleans: Garmmer Press, Inc., 1988), pp. 43-46.
4.   Garvey, ibid., p. 46.
5.   de Lavigne, op. cit., pp. 13-14.

XII. Beauregard-Keyes House

1. de Lavigne, op. cit., p. 201.
2. R. Ernest Dupuy and Trever N. Dupuy, *The Encyclopedia of Military History* (New York: Harper & Row Publishers, 1986), p. 869.
3. Ibid., p. 881.
4. de Lavigne, op. cit., pp. 198-202.
5. Mel Levitt, *A Short History of New Orleans* (San Francisco: Lexikos, 1982), pp. 128-129.
6. Winer, op. cit., p. 94.
7. Winer, op. cit., p. 95..

XIII. The Octoroon Mistress

1. In the vast majority of ghost sightings the ghosts are clothed. Seldom are ghosts reported naked.
2. Leavitt, op. cit., pp. 92-93.
3. de Lavigne, op. cit., p. 30.
4. Ibid., pp. 33-34.
5. New Orleans Times-Picayune, Sunday, 25 October 1987, p. G-3.7

XIV. The Sultan's Retreat

1. Lorena Dureau, "Sultan's House, Life with an 'Exotic Ghost,'" *The Times-Picayune*, 11 February 1979, pp. 200-ff.
2. Ibid.
3. Ibid.
4. Ibid.
5. Ibid.
6. Ibid.
7. Ibid.

XV. The Creole Lady

1. Winer, op. cit., pp. 101-108.
2. Ibid., pp. 102-103.
3. Ibid., pp. 103-108.

XVI. The Sky Is Falling

1. *Mysteries of the Unexplained* (New York: The Reader's Digest Association, Inc., 1982), pp. 184-206.
2. de Lavigne, op. cit., p. 278.
3. Ibid.
4. Saxon, op. cit., p. 285.
5. de Lavigne, op. cit., p. 279.
6. Ibid.

XVII. The Family Ghost

1. Information obtained through a telephone interview with the subject.
2. A belief voiced by the subject.
3. Documentation on file in the author's private records.

XVIII. Gallows' Trap

1. This is the tale of a legend that has been a part of the New Orleans Carrollton tradition since at least 1937.
2. Many an older resident swears the sound of the gallows can be heard to this day.

XIX. Destrehan Manor

1. Saxon, op. cit., p. 271.
2. *Ghost Sightings At Destrehan Plantation? . . . You Be The Judge,* Annoymous, non-copyrighted pamphlet sold at Destrehan Gift Shop, pp. 1-2.

XX. The Ghost In the Photograph

1. Joe Culotta is a local radio personality, chemistry instructor, adult education instructor, astrologer, searcher for the truth and a personal friend for approximately 15 years.

XXI. The Legacy of Marie Laveau

1. Information obtained through a National Parks Service Tour of St. Louis Cemetery No. 1.

2. Ibid.

3. Source accessed through Tulane University's Louisiana Collection.

4. Herbert Asbury, *The French Quarter* (New York: Garden City Publishing Co., Inc., 1938), pp. 256-257.

5. Eliphas Levi, *The Key of the Mysteries* (London: Rider & Company, 1969), p. 26.

6. Cemetery Tour op. cit.

7. Winer, etc., op cit., pp. 79-80.

XXII. Epilogue

1. Spense, op. cit., pp. 330-332.

2. Cohen, op. cit., p. 13.

3. Colin Wilson, *Mysteries*, (New York, New York: G. P. Putnam's Sons, 1980), pp. 65-67.

4. Thomas Lethbridge, *Ghost and Ghoul*, (London: Routhlege & Kegan, Ltd., 1961), p. 10 ff.

5. de Lavigne, op. cit., p. ix.
   Winer and Osborn, op. cit., p. 93.
   Saxon, op. cit., p. 279.

6. Spence, op. cit., pp. 325-326.

7. Bronislaw Malinowski, Magic, *Science and Religion*, (Garden City, New York: Doubleday Anchor Books, 1954), pp. 14-23.

8. Stephen Hawkin, *A Brief History of Time*, (Toranto, New York, New York, etc.: Bantam Books, 1988), pp. 159-162.

Bibliography

Asbury, Herbert. *The French Quarter*, Garden City, New York: Garden City Publishing Co., Inc., 1936.

Ball, Millie. "Historic Haunts: A Halloween Visit With Ghosts in the Quarter." *The Times Picayune*, Sunday, October 25, 1989, pp. G-3 and G-5.

Campbell, Joseph, with Moyers, Bill. *The Power of Myth*, lst ed. New York: Doubleday, 1988.

Cohen, Daniel. *In Search of Ghosts*, lst ed. New York, New York: Dodd, Mead and Company, 1972.

Cowan, Walter G., et al. *New Orleans: Yesterday and Today*, 1st ed. Baton Rouge, La.: Louisiana State University Press, 1983.

Crescent Books. *New Orleans: A Picture Book to Remember Her By*, New York, New York: Crown Publishers, Inc., 1978.

deLavigne, Jeanne. *Ghost Stories of Old New Orleans*, New York: Rinehart and Co., Inc., 1946.

Dupuy, Ernest R. and Traver N. Dupuy. *The Encyclopedia of Military History - from 3500 B.C. to the Present*, 2nd revised ed. New York, New York: Harper and Row, Publishers, 1986.

Dureau, Lorena. "Sultan's House: Life with an Exotic Ghost." *The Times Picayune*, Sunday, February 11, 1979, pp. 20-ff.

Foster, Mary. "Spook Houses." *The Times Picayune*, Saturday, October 31, 1987.

Fuller, Margaret. "Drops of Blood . . ." *The Times Picayune*, Saturday, November, 10, 1979.

Gandolfo, Henri A. *Metairie Cemetary: An Historical Memoir*, New Orleans: Stewart Enterprises, Inc. 1981.

Garvey, John B. and Mary Lou Garvey. *Beautiful Crescent: A History of New Orleans*, 3rd ed., New Orleans: Garmor Press, Inc., 1984.

Ghost Sightings At Destrehan Plantation, Annoymous, non-copyrighted pamphlet produced at Destrehan Plantation, Destrehan, Louisiana.

Grolier, Incorporated. *Encyclopedia International*, New York, New York: Grolier, Incorporated, 1970.

Hawking, Stephen W. *A Brief History of Time*, Toronto, New York: Bantham Books, 1988.

Holzer, Hans. *Gothic Ghosts*, New York: The Bobbs-Merrill Company, Inc., 1980.

Huber, Leonard V. *New Orleans: A Pictorial History*, New York: Crown Publishers, Inc. 1975.

Leavitt, Mel. *A Short History of New Orleans*, San Francisco: Lexikos, 1982.

Great Characters of New Orleans, San Francisco: Lexikos, 1984.

Lethbridge, Thomas. *Ghost and Ghoul*, London: Routledge & Kegan, Ltd., 1961.

Levi, Eliphas. *The Key of the Mysteries*, London: Rider and Company, 1969.

Malinowski, Bronislaw. *Magic, Science and Religion*, Garden City, New York: Doubleday Anchor Books, 1954.

Myers, Arthur. *The Ghostly Register*, New York: Contemporary Books, Inc., 1986.

Reader's Digest. *Mysteries of the Unexplained*, Pleasantville, N.Y.: The Reader's Digest Association, Inc., 1982.

Roberts, Bruce and Nancy Roberts. *America's Most Haunted Places*, Garden City, New York: Doubleday and Company, Inc., 1976.

Saxon, Lyle, and Robert Tallant. *Gumbo Ya-Ya*, Louisiana Writers Project Publishers, 3rd series. Cambridge, Mass.: The Riverside Press, 1945.

Spence, Lewis. *An Encyclopedia of Occultism,* New York: University Books, 1960.

Stanforth, Dierdre, and Louis Reems. *Romantic New Orleans,* New York: The Viking Press, 1977.

Stouse, Suzanne. "Tales to Tell on Halloween." *The Times Picayune,* Sunday, October 28, 1979.

Taylor, John Gray. *Louisiana A Bicentennial History,* New York: W.W. Norton and Company, 1976.

Wilson, Colin. *Mysteries,* 1st Perigre Printing, New York: Dodd, Mead and Company, 1972.

Winer, Richard and Nancy Osborn. *Haunted Houses,* 7th printing, New York: Bantam Books, Inc., 1980.

Index